Charles Seale-Hayne Library
University of Plymouth
(01752) 588 588
LibraryandITenquiries@plymouth.ac.uk

WORKING MEMORY AND THINKING

Working Memory and Thinking

edited by

Robert H. Logie and Kenneth J. Gilhooly
University of Aberdeen, Scotland, UK

Psychology Press
a member of the Taylor & Francis group

© 1998 by Psychology Press Ltd, a member
of the Taylor and Francis group.

Psychology Press Ltd
27 Church Road
Hove
East Sussex, BN2 3FA
UK

British Library Cataloguing in Publication Data

A catalogue record for this book is available from the British Library

ISBN 0–86377–514–4 (Hbk)

Phototypeset by Intype London Ltd
Printed and bound in the United Kingdom by Biddles Ltd,
Guildford and King's Lynn

Contents

Contributors

Andrew R.A. Conway, Department of Psychology, University of Illinois, Chicago, Illinois 60607–7137, USA.

Peter F. Delaney, Department of Psychology, Florida State University, Tallahassee, Florida 32306–1270, USA.

Sergio Della Sala, Department of Psychology, University of Aberdeen, Old Aberdeen AB24 2UB, UK.

Randall W. Engle, School of Psychology, Georgia Institute of Technology, Atlanta, Georgia 30332–0170, USA.

K. Anders Ericsson, Department of Psychology, Florida State University, Tallahassee, Florida 32306–1270, USA.

Mark J. Forshaw, School of Health and Social Sciences, Coventry University, Priory Street, Coventry CV1 5FB, UK.

Kenneth J. Gilhooly, Department of Psychology, University of Aberdeen, Old Aberdeen AB24 2UB, UK.

Graeme S. Halford, Department of Psychology, University of Queensland, Queensland 4072, Australia.

Robert H. Logie, Department of Psychology, University of Aberdeen, Old Aberdeen AB24 2UB, UK.

Louise H. Phillips, Department of Psychology, University of Aberdeen, Old Aberdeen AB24 2UB, UK.

Pertti Saariluoma, Department of Cognitive Science, 00014 University of Helsinki, Helsinki, Finland.

CHAPTER ONE

Thinking in Working Memory

Kenneth J. Gilhooly and Robert H. Logie
University of Aberdeen, Scotland, UK

Thinking and memory are inextricably linked. However a "divide-and-rule" approach has led cognitive psychologists to study these two areas in relative isolation. The present volume aims to break down the scientific divisions and foster scientific integration in the connections between these two core functions of cognition. We define thinking broadly as mentally driven change in current representations. The processes involved in such change would include application of logical rules, heuristics, strategies typically aimed at solving problems, making decisions, planning, and comprehension of complex material. Memory involves the encoding, retention, and retrieval of information, and the retention may be temporary or in a long-term knowledge base. Thinking cannot occur in a vacuum; it relies on the long-term knowledge base and a temporary workspace. Each chapter in this volume addresses different aspects of the interaction between thinking and differing conceptions of the mental temporary workspace known as working memory. The chapters by Gilhooly, Phillips and Forshaw, Della Sala and Logie, and Saariluoma espouse the multiple-component view of working memory in which different task demands are met by differing, specialised working-memory components (Baddeley, 1986). Each component then draws on relevant information in the long-term knowledge base. Engle sits astride the multiple-component view of working memory and the dominant North American "modal model" of a single flexible resource for differing forms of processing and storage. Both Halford, and Ericsson and Delaney focus on the development of knowledge structures. In the

1

case of Halford these knowledge structures incorporate a form of "conceptual chunking", which develops as children grow to maturity, and enhances the efficiency with which working memory can operate. Ericsson and Delaney discuss how the development of expert knowledge in adults permits ease of access to knowledge within the domains of expertise.

Thinking is constrained by the content, nature, and organisation of the knowledge base. It is also constrained by the ease with which information from the knowledge base and the environment can be retrieved, and then maintained and processed within working memory. The operation of working memory is constrained by its architecture, and the efficiency of operations within that architecture. A dramatic example of the interaction between thinking and the architecture of the temporary workspace is provided by the contrast between natural and artificial "thinkers". At the time of writing (May 1997), the world champion human chess player Kasparov is locked in battle with "Deep Blue", an artificial chess-playing opponent, which has essentially unlimited workspace. These opponents appear very closely matched in performance (although Deep Blue prevailed), yet the underlying architecture and concomitant strategies (or processes of "thinking") are vastly different. Less dramatically, Broadbent (1993) has noted that artificial intelligence systems for problem-solving generally require manifestly larger workspace than that available to human problem-solvers. An equally striking feature of human thinking emerges from the ability to deal with more than one task demand at a time. Humans can drive a car and hold a conversation, or store partial solutions while tackling other aspects of a problem. Current trends in air-traffic volume place multiple processing and storage demands on air-traffic controllers, and yet air travel remains one of the safest forms of transportation. These apparent paradoxes, as to how humans can be such successful thinkers despite their very limited working memory, present significant scientific challenges.

Gilhooly addresses the role of working memory in reasoning tasks. A number of studies, using dual-task methodology, indicate that central executive and articulatory loop components are typically involved in reasoning tasks. It is noted that "reasoning tasks" are more often than not solved by heuristic strategies that differ from strict reasoning. It is argued that in order fully to understand how strategies for solving problems are implemented, the demands that the strategy implementations place on working-memory components must be specified. Examples are developed of the ways in which alternative implementations of the same strategy may place greater and lesser loads on working-memory components. From studies of response patterns and thinking-aloud records, for instance, it is possible to identify the broad strategy followed. From studies of working-memory component loadings, it is possible to gain information on how the major strategy is implemented.

The issue of strategies arises again in studies of working memory and ageing in reasoning tasks, as discussed in the chapter by Phillips and Forshaw. The difficulty in establishing clear links between measures of working-memory characteristics, age, and performance in a range of tasks may be caused by subjects adopting strategies that compensate for reduced working-memory capacities by minimising loads on working memory while still yielding a satisfactory level of performance. Phillips and Forshaw point out the many problems of reliability and validity that arise from attempts to measure individual differences in working-memory capacities and processing efficiency.

Phillips and Forshaw argue that although the link between working memory and ageing is not completely resolved, the age effects that have been reported might be attributable largely to changes in processing speed with age. The underlying neurological changes that occur in normal ageing are somewhat modest compared with those suffered by patients with brain damage as a result of injury, disease, stroke, tumour, or neurosurgery. Disorders of thinking ought to accompany neurological damage. However, in their chapter, Della Sala and Logie note that although gross cognitive impairments are observed in brain-damaged patients, disorders of thinking are not clearly understood. In large part, this stems from which functions of cognition might be considered to fall under the umbrella of "thinking", with many researchers in neuropsychology preferring to refer to impairments in "executive functions". The issue is further complicated by the reference in this literature to "frontal functions", linking executive aspects of cognition with the functioning of the frontal lobes, a link that is by no means clear cut. Nevertheless, the area is ripe for exploration both with respect to the understanding of the effects of brain damage, and with respect to the implications that neuropsychological findings have for our understanding of thinking in the healthy brain.

The chapter by Engle and Conway incorporates some aspects of the multiple-component model of working memory, but largely consigns the "slave systems" of working memory (phonological loop and visuo-spatial sketch-pad) to relatively minor roles in language comprehension. Much of the focus of their chapter is on individual differences in working-memory span and its association with individual variability in comprehension. They conclude that the executive component of working memory probably contributes little to much of everyday skilled comprehension. Working memory, then, is only brought to bear when comprehension tasks involve complex syntax or ongoing interruptions.

Engle's contribution to the literature has focused on the activation of stored knowledge of semantics and syntax in order to deal with comprehension tasks. Much of this access, then, is automated in skilled comprehension. This theme arises in the Ericsson and Delaney chapter in their discussion of "long-term working memory". The issue here is that as expertise is acquired in particular domains, that expertise, in the form of stored knowledge, becomes readily available for performing tasks relevant to the expertise. Experts can then demonstrate on-line processing and storage capacity far in excess of the typically reported limits for working memory, particularly in thinking and problem-solving. The authors build on the proposal of Ericsson and Kintsch (1995) that experts develop efficient encoding and retrieval schemes that enable them rapidly to store relevant new information in long-term memory and retrieve it rapidly as needed in the course of solving problems. Effectively, expert solvers have an extended long-term working memory to supplement short-term working memory. Persuasive evidence is adduced from studies of expert chess players, mnemonists, medical diagnosticians, and skilled readers.

Saariluoma focuses on the role of working memory in the adversary problem domain of chess. Applying the multiple-component model of working memory, Saariluoma presents evidence that the visuo-spatial sketch-pad and central executive are crucially involved in chess play. Saariluoma also points to the role of long-term working memory as proposed by Ericsson and Delaney in their chapter. Long-term working memory has a role in normal chess play as a store for alternative move sequences ("episodes"), which are generated as the player explores possible moves and decides between the options generated. The ability of experts to engage successfully in simultaneous blindfold play of 10 or more games is a dramatic example of long-term working memory in action.

The effects of developing an expert knowledge base, discussed both by Ericsson and Delaney, and by Saariluoma, recur in a different form in the chapter by Halford. As children grow older, Halford argues, they develop conceptual knowledge, which allows them to simplify complex relations and associations. In a manner that echoes the development of expert skill in adults, children develop skills in conceptual chunking, thereby making better use of limited processing capacity. The apparent increase in processing capacity on the way to adulthood arises, then, from an ability to simplify.

The chapters herein represent a diversity of views as regards the nature of working memory. They also cover diverse forms of human thinking. In so doing, the links between working memory and thinking are directly addressed and made explicit. By bringing together a range of views and current research on the nature of the links, we hope that this volume will contribute to an increasingly integrated understanding of human thinking and memory.

REFERENCES

Baddeley, A.D. (1986). *Working memory.* Oxford: Oxford University Press.

Broadbent, D.E. (1993). Comparison with human experiments. In D.E. Broadbent (Ed.), *The simulation of human intelligence* (pp. 198–217). Oxford: Blackwell.

Ericsson, K.A., & Kintsch, W. (1995). Long term working memory. *Psychological Review, 102,* 211–245.

CHAPTER TWO

Working Memory, Strategies, and Reasoning Tasks

Kenneth J. Gilhooly
University of Aberdeen, Scotland, UK

1. INTRODUCTION

In life, memory and thinking are inextricably intertwined. When tackling a problem, previously acquired concepts must be retrieved from long-term memory to represent the problem situation, previously acquired rules in long-term memory need to be activated to change the problem representation towards the goal state, intermediate results may need to be held briefly in working memory, and the results of thought may in turn change long-term memory contents. The present chapter will be focusing particularly on the interrelations between working memory and that form of thinking referred to as reasoning. The role of working memory in reasoning was a concern of the originating papers of the Baddeley–Hitch working-memory model (Baddeley & Hitch, 1974; Hitch & Baddeley, 1976) and this concern continues. In common with many of the chapters in this book, I will be discussing the issues within the framework of the Baddeley–Hitch model of working memory as a tripartite system consisting of central executive, phonological (or articulatory) loop, and visuo-spatial scratch-pad (or sketch-pad). In the remainder of this section I will consider various questions of definition that gather around the notion of "reasoning" and its associate "rationality", then, in the second section, I will outline salient empirical results, and in the last section, I will develop a theoretical discussion of how working memory and strategies for reasoning tasks could interact.

Firstly, how might "thinking" be defined? I propose that "thinking" is an internally driven process of changing the currently active mental representation. It is plausible to suppose that the currently active mental representation is maintained in working memory. So, thinking is a process of changing currently active mental representations held in working memory.

Second, how might "reasoning" be defined as a special type of thinking process? A recent definition of reasoning is: "When most psychologists talk about 'reasoning' they mean an explicit sequential thought process of some kind, consisting of propositional representations" (Evans & Over, 1996, p. 15). This definition is helpful in stressing that reasoning is an *explicit* rather than an implicit process and is *sequential* rather than parallel. However, this definition, as it stands, is possibly over-inclusive, and could apply to most cases of problem-directed thinking. For this chapter, I will limit "reasoning", as a form of thinking, to explicit sequential thought processes that are effectively equivalent to the application of a sequence of rules of some formal system. Formal systems provide sets of general rules for reaching correct conclusions from given statements.

The principal formal systems are those of deductive logic, mathematics, statistics, probability, decision theory and, although less fully formalised, inductive and deontic logics. Such theories are couched in abstract terms and can apply to a wide variety of contents for which the appropriate relationships hold (such as set inclusion, exclusion, overlap, implication, negation, and so on). Thus, reasoning involves the application of very general rules to specific contents.

Reasoning *tasks*, then, can be defined as tasks that could be successfully tackled by the application of a formal theory and require no real-world knowledge of the objects being reasoned about. However, presentation of a reasoning task is no guarantee that reasoning will be evoked. Indeed, it is a recurrent theme in research on reasoning tasks that subjects generally do *not* actually reason! Instead, a wide variety of heuristic *strategies* have been postulated as underlying performance in reasoning tasks, and such strategies, although generally superior in results to guessing, are typically not equivalent to logical rule application. The hypothesis that subjects respond to syllogisms, for example, by reasoning correctly, is plainly wrong; the modal answer to most syllogisms is an error of some sort (Erickson, 1978). Indeed, the frequency of errors in reasoning tasks has been taken by some as having bleak implications for human rationality (Cohen, 1981; Sutherland, 1992). Because reasoning, in the sense defined above, is not modal even in response to reasoning tasks, this chapter would be rather brief if it focused solely on working memory and thinking that was equivalent to logical rule application. Instead, this chapter will address the role of working memory in reasoning *tasks*, and consider how that role may vary with different strategies and different tasks.

Finally, in this section, let us consider definitions of "rationality". Because reasoning in the sense of logic-equivalent processes seems to be rare, it is tempting to conclude that humans are irrational. However, on the other hand humans are a very successful species and have constructed those very logical systems against which their own thinking can be assessed, as well as building enormously complex and highly effective physical systems, such as computers and space rockets; these achievements suggest rationality rather than irrationality. Alternative routes to reconcile the apparently conflicting evidence on human rationality have been espoused. Firstly, there is the idea of "bounded rationality" (Simon, 1978), which proposes that humans can apply rules of reasoning but only within capacity limits—and among these limits working-memory limits are very important. Because of capacity limits, certain heuristics, which sacrifice some accuracy in order to save mental overload, are followed. In terms of "optimality" (Anderson, 1991), use of such heuristics may maximise utility when cognitive-effort costs are included and so be "rational", whereas use of correct reasoning rules may be suboptimal when effort costs are taken into account and so be "irrational".

Another line of defence of human rationality is to argue that humans (and other species) may show "adaptive rationality" (Anderson, 1991; Evans & Over, 1996) and achieve important goals by means of *implicit* learning processes that fine-tune behaviour to match environmental regularities. The behaviour of bees, for example, may conform to the predictions of optimal search theories, but it seems safe to assume that bees do not actually work through these rules explicitly. Rather, through a combination of evolutionary pre-wiring and simple learning processes, their behaviour becomes adapted to their environment with good results. Adaptively, rational mechanisms do not involve explicit strategic processes and so would not be expected to load working memory. Evans and Over (1996) label explicit reasoning processes as showing rationality$_1$, whereas implicitly rational processes are labelled as showing rationality$_2$. They suggest that many "errors" in reasoning tasks are due to elicitation of implicit rational processes rather than explicit rational processes. Stevenson (in press) points out a third option, which is that heuristic strategies that are explicit may also be elicited (i.e. not all explicit processes will be strictly equivalent to reasoning with formal rules of logic). It is quite possible that tasks designed to evoke explicit reasoning will tend to evoke explicit heuristic strategies that perform below the level of correct reasoning (but load working memory) or implicit adaptive processes, which may deliver a fast response with no loading of working memory. The following sections of this chapter focus on the possible role of working memory and its components in tasks designed to evoke reasoning, with special reference to differences among strategies.

2. WORKING MEMORY IN REASONING TASKS: EMPIRICAL RESULTS

2.1 The AB task

In Baddeley and Hitch's (1974) seminal presentation on working memory, considerable emphasis is given to studies of the role of working memory in reasoning, and these studies were also reported in greater detail in Hitch and Baddeley (1976). The experiments in question involved the use of a task known as the AB task (Baddeley, 1968), in which the subject is presented with sentences that claim to describe the order of two letters at the end of each sentence and the subject must indicate as quickly as possible whether each sentence is true or false. For example, given "A does not precede B-AB", the subject should response "False". The sentences varied in terms of being positive or negative, active or passive, true or false, and in letter order (AB, BA), and whether the term "follows" or "precedes" was used. The question may arise as to whether this is truly a task of "reasoning" as against a task of "comprehension". Analysis of the task may be helpful at this point. A plausible task analysis of the AB problem is that subjects infer from the sentence what the order of letters would be if the sentence were true and determine whether the predicted order matches the obtained order. This would involve converting negatives to positives, e.g. from "does not precede" to "follows", and passives into actives, e.g. from "A is followed by B" to "B follows A". By applying such conversion rules, an initial sentence can be converted into an affirmative active sentence and a predicted order can be derived for direct comparison with the actual order. This analysis is similar to that proposed by Clark and Chase (1972) for the process of comparing sentences against pictures. Baddeley and Hitch's control results (1974, Fig. 1, p. 54) show that the active affirmative sentences are processed fastest, then passive affirmative, active negative, and passive negative. The active v. passive and affirmative v. negative factors had independent effects on latencies. These control data are consistent with the sequential task analysis just outlined. It seems reasonable, then, to conclude that the AB task does involve explicit sequential processes that involve formal rules of affirmative–negative and active–passive transformation.

Accepting that the AB task is a reasoning task, what emerged regarding the role of working memory from these early studies? Firstly, pre-loads of up to six digits could be successfully maintained with no effects on reasoning speed or accuracy. However, when six-item pre-loads had to be articulated concurrently with the reasoning task there was a marked slowing down in reasoning speed, particularly on the more difficult items. Hammerton (1969) also found a similar interfering effect of concurrent articulation (of the sentence "Mary had a little lamb") on the AB task. These data strongly suggest an involvement of the phonological loop in this reasoning task. Further support for this conclusion came from a further study reported by Baddeley and Hitch (1974), in which the letters in the task varied in phonemic and visual similarity. Phonemic similarity reduced the number of items correctly solved over a large set of problems, but there was no effect of visual similarity (suggesting no strong role for the visuo-spatial scratch-pad in this task). A subsequent study by Farmer, Berman, and Fletcher (1986) found a marked effect of articulatory suppression (repeating "1234" as fast as possible) on AB task speed and errors, but no effect of a spatial suppression task (repeatedly tapping four keys in order). These data are consistent with those of Baddeley and Hitch (1974), and Hammerton (1969) in suggesting that the AB task involves the phonological loop but not the visuo-spatial scratch-pad.

2.2 Propositional reasoning

Given as premises "If p then q" and "p", what follows? The valid (modus ponens) inference is "q". Given "If p then q" and "not-q", "not-p" follows validly (modus tollens). Given "If p then q" and "not-p" (denial of the antecedent) or "q" (affirmation of the consequent) nothing validly follows. These problems are examples of conditional reasoning and represent basic problems in propositional logic. Two broad theoretical approaches that indicate rather different strategies for tackling such problems are the mental models (Johnson-Laird & Byrne, 1991) and the mental rules approaches (Braine, 1978; Rips, 1994). The mental-models approach explains task difficulty in terms of the number of mental models that must be generated and evaluated to test possible conclusions, whereas the rules approaches offer explanations in terms of the number of steps in a mental logic that must be applied to move from premises to conclusion. Both approaches propose that working memory can be overloaded, by models or by rules, and that working-memory loading is a major cause of error. The use of secondary tasks in conditional reasoning has been explored in order to test and sharpen this hypothesis, and the salient results will now be outlined (Evans & Brooks, 1981; Toms, Morris, & Ward, 1993; Klauer, Stegmaier, & Meiser, 1997).

Evans and Brooks (1981) applied methods similar to those of Hitch and Baddeley (1976) in conditional reasoning tasks and found no evidence of central-executive or articulatory-loop involvement. However, as Halford, Bain, and Maybery argued (1985), the Evans and Brooks experiments may have been insensitive, owing to use of secondary tasks that imposed too low a concurrent load. Also, they did not check for trading-off, so the null results could reflect attentional focus on the main task at the expense of the secondary tasks. Toms et al. (1994) addressed questions similar to those posed by Evans and Brooks, but made use of more thoroughly pre-tested secondary tasks. Subjects in Toms et al.'s studies carried out conditional inference tasks with and without secondary tapping, tracking, articulation, and memory loads. Neither tracking nor tapping affected conditional inference performance, suggesting no role for the visuo-spatial scratch-pad in this task. Although articulatory suppression did not affect conditional inferences, memory load did have a detrimental effect, particularly on modus tollens problems. The memory load and articulation conditions were similar in that articulation involved repeating the digits 1–6 over and over at a rate of 2 digits per sec, whereas the memory-load condition involved a different random order of digits 1–6 per trial, which were to be repeated aloud at a rate of 2 digits per sec. The additional load of recalling random sequences rather than the overlearned sequence appears to have been critical in bringing about an interfering effect on the main task. Further, the concurrent memory-load task was also shown to interfere with a spatial-memory task (which was also disrupted by concurrent tapping but not by articulatory suppression). Overall, Toms et al. concluded that conditional reasoning did not involve the visuo-spatial scratch-pad or articulatory loop, but required some abstract working-memory medium for representation, which could be provided by the central executive. A cautionary note that may be made here, regarding the null results, is that Toms et al. did not check for possible trade-offs. Subjects may have maintained inference performance at the cost of concurrent articulation and tapping performance, thus giving the impression that visuo-spatial scratch-pad and articulatory loop were not involved, if only inference performance is examined. A further reservation is that the conclusion regarding the central executive is somewhat indirect, as secondary tasks that clearly load the central executive, such as random generation, were not used.

To a large extent, the questions raised here regarding Toms et al.'s study were tackled in research by Klauer, Stegmaier, and Meiser (1997). They investigated a range of propositional reasoning tasks involving conditionals, biconditionals, and exclusive and inclusive disjunctions with a range of secondary tasks and included checks for trading-off. The basic results indicated small interfering effects of articulatory suppression, marked interference of verbal random generation and no interference from visual tracking on propositional reasoning. In the other direction, propositional reasoning had marked effects on random generation, did not disrupt articulatory suppression, but did have a mildly impairing effect on visual tracking. Thus, it may be inferred that propositional reasoning strongly involves the central executive, with lesser roles for the articulatory loop and visuo-spatial scratch-pad. However, this conclusion may only hold when subjects are untrained. Klauer et al. surmised that: (1) untrained subjects may tend to apply (implicit) heuristics, which impose only a relatively low load on working memory slave components; and (2) that training in considering the possible truth values of the terms in the rules would induce a more analytic approach, similar to that envisaged by mental models theory (Johnson-Laird & Byrne, 1991). A suitable training method was devised, and after successful plotting was used as pre-training in a study involving tapping as a secondary task. The propositional reasoning of subjects with pre-training was indeed more disrupted by tapping than that of untrained subjects. Neither group showed any trading-off between primary and secondary tasks. It was concluded that use of a mental model-like strategy involved loading the visuo-spatial scratch-pad. Thus, a further conclusion from Klauer et al. is that the pattern of loading of working memory in a task depends on the strategy applied to the task. Further evidence on the interplay between patterns of working-memory loading and strategies comes from studies carried out in our laboratory on syllogistic reasoning, and these studies will be described and discussed in the following sections.

2.3 Syllogistic reasoning tasks

The area of *syllogistic reasoning* (see, e.g. Evans, Newstead, & Byrne, 1994, for a review) is particularly attractive for the present purposes in that a number of theorists have specifically proposed an involvement of working memory in syllogistic task performance (Sternberg & Turner, 1981; Fisher, 1981; Johnson-Laird, 1983; Johnson-Laird & Byrne, 1991). Syllogistic arguments invite reasoning about category relationships and involve two statements (premises) assumed true; for example, "All dogs are mammals" and "All corgis are dogs". One premise relates the subject of the argument (corgis) to the middle term (dogs), and the other premise relates the middle term to the predicate (mammals). The types of relationships between subject, middle, and predicate terms used in syllogistic arguments are those of set inclusion, overlap, and exclusion, *viz.*, all, some, none, some not. The subjects' task is to indicate what conclusion, if any, can be drawn relating the subject and predicate terms to one another. In the earlier example, it can be validly inferred that "All corgis are mammals". The number of possible syllogistic argument structures is quite large. Because each of the two premises can involve any one of four logical relations, there are 16 such combinations. Furthermore, there are four possible ways, known as "figures", in which the subject, predicate, and middle terms can be arranged in the two premises.

Combining the 4 possible figures with the 16 possible combinations of logical relations yields 64 logically distinct argument forms. Interestingly, some argument forms are almost invariably handled correctly and some almost always lead to error. For example, taking two syllogisms that differ in both figure and the type of relations used, Johnson-Laird and Bara (1984) found that 19 out of their 20 subjects correctly solved the syllogism "All A are B; All B are C; Therefore?" (Answer: "All A are C"); while none out of 20 solved "Some B are not A; All B are C; Therefore?" (Answer: "Some C are not A"). Despite over 60 years of experimental and theoretical study (e.g. Begg & Denny, 1969; Ford, 1995; Johnson-Laird & Bara, 1984; Polk & Newell, 1995; Stenning & Oberlander, 1995; Wetherick & Gilhooly, 1995; Wilkins, 1928; Woodworth & Sells, 1935), there is still no generally agreed account of how people process such arguments. Many accounts agree that working-memory load is a major factor in causing difficulty (e.g. Fisher, 1981; Johnson-Laird, 1983; Sternberg & Turner, 1981), but rather few studies have addressed the detailed involvement of working memory in syllogistic reasoning paradigms.

As already indicated, studies of working memory involvement in non-syllogistic reasoning (Baddeley & Hitch, 1974; Evans & Brooks, 1981; Farmer et al., 1986; Hitch & Baddeley, 1976; Klauer et al., 1997) have tended to find small effects of articulatory suppression and large effects of central-executive loading tasks. In the case of syllogisms, Gilhooly, Logie, Wetherick, and Wynn (1993) reported two experiments. In the first, working-memory load was varied by presenting syllogistic tasks either verbally (causing a high memory load) or visually (so that the premises were continuously available for inspection and memory load was low). A significant effect of memory load on accuracy of syllogistic performance was obtained. In the second experiment, both premises were simultaneously presented visually for a subject-determined time. Dual-task methods were used to assess the role of working-memory components. Syllogistic performance was disrupted by concurrent random-number generation, but not by concurrent articulatory suppression or by concurrent tapping in a pre-set pattern. Furthermore, the concurrent syllogism task interfered with random generation and, to a lesser extent, with articulatory suppression, but not with tapping. It was concluded that although the central executive component of working memory played a major role in the syllogistic task performance reported, the phonological loop had a lesser role and the visuo-spatial scratch-pad was not involved.

Gilhooly et al. (1993) distinguished a number of distinct strategies employed in the syllogism task. These were as follows:

1. The atmosphere strategy (Woodworth & Sells, 1935), according to

which if one premise is negative the subjects make a negative conclusion (otherwise they choose a positive conclusion); and if one
premise is particular, subjects choose a particular conclusion, otherwise a universal conclusion.

2. The matching strategy (Wetherick & Gilhooly, 1995), according to
which subjects give as the conclusion a proposition of the same
logical form as the more conservative of the premises, where the
logical forms are ordered for conservatism, from most to least, "No",
"Some not", "Some", and "All".

3. Logic-equivalent strategies—these were not specified in detail but
lead to logically correct answers to most syllogisms.

4. Guessing—in which subjects simply guess among the five alternatives
presented on each trial.

The set of syllogisms used was such that atmosphere, matching, and logic-
equivalent strategies could be identified from the response patterns. Subjects were classed according to which strategy fitted their response patterns
best. Response patterns that did not fit the other main strategies and led to
low correct rates were classed as guessing patterns. In control, articulatory
suppression, and tapping conditions the matching strategy predominated.
No significant shifting of strategy frequency occurred with tapping or
articulatory suppression. With random generation there was a marked
increase in the incidence of guessing, although even in this high-load
situation average accuracy (8.56/20) was significantly above chance levels
(4.00/20). These results indicate that varying secondary loads can bring
about changes in strategy and complement the results of Klauer et al.
(1997), who found that changing strategy (increasing strategy load)
affected the impact of a fixed secondary load (tapping).

In a follow-up study of syllogistic reasoning, Gilhooly, Logie, and Wynn
(in review) used sequential premise presentation as against simultaneous
premise presentation. Sequential presentation involves a greater storage
load, and it was expected that the slave systems would show a greater
involvement in these circumstances. Although there was no effect from
concurrent tapping on accuracy or latencies in the reasoning task with
sequential presentation, there were impairments of average tapping speed
and of consistency of tapping rate in the dual condition. These results
suggest a difficulty in performing both syllogistic reasoning and tapping
simultaneously, and therefore some involvement of the visuo-spatial
scratch-pad in the syllogism task. The articulatory-suppression conditions
showed impairment of both syllogistic accuracy and speed of conclusion
reporting, and also slowing down and greater variation in articulation
rates in the dual condition. These results support the conclusion that the
articulatory loop is heavily involved in syllogistic reasoning in this study.

Random Generation rate was significantly slower and more variable in the dual condition, and there was also a highly significant effect on reasoning task performance and a deterioration in randomness, as measured by the Evans (1978) RNG index. A plausible explanation for the mutual interference between syllogisms and random generation is the high loading the dual condition places on the central executive because of the requirement continuously to generate and select responses at the same time as processing the different elements of the syllogistic problem. The load on memory is heavy, with subjects having to maintain randomness of numbers by remembering those already generated and at the same time having to keep the syllogistic statements and the subject of the argument in memory, in order to reach a conclusion.

In terms of strategies, the atmosphere strategy was most prevalent in control, and the slave memory loads did not significantly affect strategy frequency. However, random generation, as in our earlier simultaneous premise presentation study, produced a significant increase in the percentage of subjects classed as following a guessing strategy to 56% v. 15% in control conditions. However, average accuracy, even in random generation (7.44/20), was significantly above chance levels (4.00/20). As in the simultaneous premise presentation study, varying load produced a shift in preferred strategy. Let us now compare the two presentation experiments.

With *simultaneous* display of the syllogistic argument premises throughout the premise-processing period, as in Gilhooly et al. (1993), there is a relatively light load on working memory, with subjects able to "refresh" their memory of the different elements of the problem while attempting to draw a conclusion. *Sequential* premise presentation ensures a heavier load on the slave memories, leading to mutual interference between reasoning and articulatory suppression, and interference from reasoning to tapping. The lack of memory support during the premise-processing period may incline subjects to move more rapidly to the conclusion-indicating phase, where support in the form of alternative conclusions is available. This difference in information availability may underlie the lack of sensitivity of the premise-processing time measure in the sequential study compared with simultaneous mode studies (Gilhooly et al., 1993).

However, a major portion of central-executive capacity would be taken up by the Random Generation task, and the mutual impairment of syllogistic reasoning and random generation in the present study matches the conclusion from previous simultaneous presentation studies that syllogisms place a heavy load on the central executive (Gilhooly et al., 1993). The results of the sequential presentation experiments and those of previous studies (Gilhooly et al., 1993) support the view that there is a major involvement of the central executive in syllogistic reasoning tasks, whether presentation of the premises is simultaneous or sequential. When sequential presentations are used, dual-task methods indicate a clear involvement of the phonological loop and some involvement of the visuo-spatial scratch-pad. The slave components of working memory, especially the visuo-spatial scratch-pad, are less involved, if at all, when simultaneous premise presentation is used.

Part of the motivation for our syllogism studies was to help elucidate the exact roles played by working-memory subsystems in syllogistic reasoning. It may be argued that these roles will depend (1) on the task environment (e.g. sequential v. simultaneous premise presentation); and (2) on the strategies adopted by subjects (e.g. guessing, matching, atmosphere, or a more logical strategy). If the task environment only provides limited external memory support (as with sequential premise presentation) then there tends to be greater use of the slave memories. As the materials in syllogistic studies are verbal (even if presented in written form), it is not surprising that the phonological loop appears more involved than the visuo-spatial scratch-pad system; similar differences in the roles of the slave memories have been found in other studies of verbal reasoning using non-syllogistic tasks (e.g. Baddeley & Hitch, 1974; Evans & Brooks, 1981; Farmer et al., 1986; Halford, Bain, & Maybery, 1984; Hitch & Baddeley, 1976; Toms et al., 1993).

3. WORKING MEMORY AND STRATEGIES IN REASONING: BRIDGING THE GAP

Turning now to the interrelations between strategies and working memory involvement, "strategies" are typically described at too high a level of abstraction to mesh clearly with working-memory components. There is a need to specify typical strategies in such a way that likely component loadings can be assessed. Clearly, it would be ideal if one could measure loads per strategy specification *a priori* and perhaps rule out some alternative strategies on the grounds of excessive memory demands. However, a difficulty in specifying strategies in great detail is that a strategy described at a high level can generally always be specified at more detailed levels in many alternative ways, which may have different implications for component-memory loads. Let us take syllogisms as a paradigmatic task and consider as a concrete example of a strategy the atmosphere strategy, which was very common in our syllogism results and is described in section 2.3; similar analyses could readily be carried out for the matching and logic-equivalent strategies also described in section 2.3.

Firstly, I assume that strategies, in their various specifications, can be defined as sets of rules (presumed to be stored in long-term memory). The efficiency with which different rule sets produce syllogistic conclusions will affect component memory loads in syllogistic reasoning. Thus, the "atmosphere" strategy could be implemented in at least two ways, as follows:

1. Pattern-recognition implementation of atmosphere strategy.
This implementation involves 10 rules corresponding to each possible premise pair, where premises are represented solely by the quantifiers they contain ("All, All"; "All, Some"; "All, Some not"; "All, No"; "Some, Some", and so on). Order of quantifiers within a pair is irrelevant for this strategy. For each premise pair a response is indicated by a rule. The rule would be:

   i. If premises are "All, All" then response is "All".
   ii. If premises are "All, Some" then response is "Some".
   iii. If premises are "All, Some not" then response is "Some not".
   iv. If premises are "All, None" then response is "None".
   v. If premises are "Some, Some" then response is "Some".
   vi. If premises are "Some, Some not" then response is "Some not".
   vii. If premises are "Some, None" then response is "Some not".
   viii. If premises are "Some not, Some not" then response is "Some not".
   ix. If premises are "Some not, None" then response is "Some not".
   x. If premises are "None, None" then response is "None".

2. Sequential implementation of atmosphere strategy.
This implementation involves rule sets, which first code each premise as universal or particular and as affirmative or negative, then count the number of particulars and the number of negatives in the premises, and determine the conclusion's features, depending on whether there is at least one particular or at least one negative. "Universal" premises make statements about all members of a class, *viz.,* "All are ..." or "None are ...". Particular premises make statements about some but not all members of a class, *viz.,* "Some are ...". The relevant rules would be: (1) if there is at least one particular, then the conclusion is particular; otherwise it is universal; (2) if there is at least one negative, then the conclusion is negative; otherwise it is affirmative. Finally, on the basis of the features of the conclusion, a response is determined by four rules:

   i. If conclusion is Negative-Particular, then response is "Some not".
   ii. If conclusion is Affirmative-Universal, then response is "All".
   iii. If conclusion is Negative-Universal, then response is "None".
   iv. If conclusion is Affirmative-Particular, then response is "Some".

It is plausible to suppose that the second specification (or implementation) of "atmosphere" outlined earlier, which depends on a sequence of stages with intermediate results, would place a greater load on working-memory components than the first implementation, which relies on directly recognising patterns in long-term memory. It could be that the first implementation is more typical of experienced subjects, and the second more typical of beginners using the atmosphere approach. Similar analyses of matching in terms of pattern recognition or a sequence of stages could be also offered; we do not present these analyses here, for reasons of space. The discussion of strategy implementation made here illustrates the point that linking strategies to loads on working-memory systems is not straightforward and requires detailed specification of strategies; also, it may be noted that rather different strategies in terms of response patterns may make similar loads on working-memory systems. For example, pattern-recognition versions of atmosphere and matching strategies would both impose low loads on working memory. As a final point here, it may be noted that working-memory load patterns may be used as constraints on possible strategies. If secondary tasks produce little disruption, then a strategy involving direct recognition seems more likely than a complex multistage strategy. Our syllogism results and those of other studies in verbal reasoning do typically show disruption by random generation and articulatory suppression, indicating that multistage implementations of the most common strategies are probably being followed, rather than "one step" pattern-recognition implementations.

Given a particular strategy specified as a particular rule set, stored in long-term memory, the following question can still be asked, "How in detail might that strategy interact with working memory components?" We will outline a rather general answer that could apply to any strategy defined as a rule set. The discussion assumes that the standard production-system model of cognitive science is a useful working framework within which to tackle the question (e.g. Meyer & Kieras, 1997; Simon & Kaplan, 1989).

Let us first consider the central-executive component. A way of linking the central executive to strategies is to suppose that the central executive plays a role akin to that of the current database in a production system and the strategies are essentially sets of production rules. Production rules are of the form "If condition A is true in the current database, then carry out action B". The conditions and actions can be quite complex; actions can involve internal information processing as well as external behaviour.

It is proposed that the central executive holds information important for current action, such as, the results of the last processing cycle, the input to the next cycle, the current goal, and the current instruction label. Processing is assumed to be carried out by rules in long-term memory that respond to central-executive contents. In other words, rules deliver new results at time $n + 1$ to the central executive, in response to the state of stored information in the central executive at time n, the time of rule application. Thus, the "central executive" holds information relevant for immediate processing and the results of recent processing. In other words, the "central executive" is not the active homunculus its name suggests, but rather a key storage site for currently important information; the actual processing work is done unconsciously by the firing of rules in long-term memory. It is surmised that "housekeeping" rules are activated to recode intermediate results to the slave memory systems, when necessary, to avoid overload and to back up the central executive system. That is, the slave systems operate as temporary "cache" memories (Logie, 1995). It seems plausible that information in the central executive is in an abstract propositional code, whereas information in slave systems is in more literal, surface-based codes (Toms et al., 1993). It may also be surmised that important information for later use during an extended task is recoded into long-term memory (cf. Ericsson & Kintsch's, 1995, long-term working-memory notion in expert problem-solving).

Turning to the slave systems, we suggest that when syllogisms are presented sequentially, these systems may hold premises in articulatory form (the phonological loop) or as visual images (visuo-spatial scratch-pad). These systems may also hold intermediate results (e.g. the two quantifiers for certain implementations of atmosphere or matching strategies; or rearranged premises for some more logic-like approaches, which may require premises such as "All Ms are Ps; Some Ss are Ms" to be reordered to "Some Ss are Ms; All Ms are Ps", in order to facilitate premise combination yielding "Some Ss are Ps"). Generally, the results of a range of studies reviewed in section 2 indicate that verbal-reasoning tasks, such as syllogisms, mainly involve the phonological loop, with only limited involvement of the visuo-spatial scratch-pad.

To sum up: the data reviewed here are consistent with a general interpretation of reasoning tasks as involving a range of strategies, each of which may be implemented in various ways and cause a range of loading patterns on working memory. More specifically, the syllogistic response patterns indicate that atmosphere and matching strategies are most common and the patterns of working-memory disruption indicate that multistage implementations of these strategies are most likely, as against one-step pattern-recognition-based implementations. Central-executive loading seems to be invariable in reasoning tasks. Finally, the way in which task information is made available (e.g. sequential presentation of premises) will affect the use made of the "slave" or "cache" memories. Of these, the phonological loop seems to be particularly important in reasoning.

REFERENCES

Anderson, J.R. (1991). Is human cognition adaptive? *Behavioural and Brain Sciences, 14*, 471–517.

Baddeley, A.D. (1968). A three-minute reasoning test based on grammatical transformation. *Psychonomic Science, 10*, 341–342.

Baddeley, A.D., & Hitch, G.J. (1974). Working memory. In G. Bower (Ed.), *Recent advances in learning and motivation: Vol. VIII* (pp. 47–90). New York: Academic Press.

Begg, I., & Denny, J.P. (1969). Empirical reconciliation of atmosphere and conversion interpretations of syllogistic reasoning errors. *Journal of Experimental Psychology, 81*, 351–354.

Braine, M.D.S. (1978). On the relation between the natural logic of reasoning and standard logic. *Psychological Review, 85*, 1–21.

Clark, H.H., & Chase, W.G. (1972). On the process of comparing sentences against pictures. *Cognitive Psychology, 3*, 372–517.

Cohen, L.J. (1981). Can human irrationality be experimentally demonstrated? *Behavioral and Brain Sciences, 4*, 317–331.

Erickson, J.R. (1978). Research in syllogistic reasoning. In R. Revlin and R. E. Meyer (Eds.), *Human reasoning* (pp. 39–40). Washington, DC: Winston.

Ericsson, K.A., & Kintsch, W. (1995). Long-term working memory. *Psychological Review, 102*, 211–245.

Evans, F.J. (1978). Monitoring attention deployment by random number generation: An index to measure subjective randomness. *Bulletin of the Psychonomic Society, 12*, 35–38.

Evans, J.St.B.T., & Brooks, P.G. (1981). Competing with reasoning: A test of the working memory hypothesis. *Current Psychological Research, 1*, 139–147.

Evans, J.St.B.T., Newstead, S.E., & Byrne, R. (1994). *Human reasoning: The psychology of deduction*. Hove: Lawrence Erlbaum Associates Ltd.

Evans, J.St.B.T., & Over, D. (1996). *Rationality and reasoning*. Hove: Psychology Press.

Farmer, E.W., Berman, J.V.F., & Fletcher, Y.L. (1986). Evidence for a visuo-spatial scratch-pad in working memory. *Quarterly Journal of Experimental Psychology, 38A*, 675–688.

Fisher, D.L. (1981). A three-factor model of syllogistic reasoning: The study of isolable stages. *Memory and Cognition, 9*, 496–514.

Ford, M. (1995). Two modes of mental representation and problem solution in syllogistic reasoning. *Cognition, 54*, 1–71.

Gilhooly, K.J., Logie, R.H., Wetherick, N.E., & Wynn, V. (1993). Working memory and strategies in syllogistic reasoning tasks. *Memory and Cognition, 21*, 115–124.

Gilhooly, K.J. Logie, R.H., & Wynn, V. (in review). Syllogistic reasoning tasks and working memory: evidence from sequential presentation of premises.

Halford, G.S., Bain, J.D., & Maybery, M.T. (1984). Does a concurrent memory load interfere with reasoning? *Current Psychological Research and Reviews, 3*, 14–23.

Hammerton, M. (1969). Interference between low information verbal output and a cognitive task. *Nature, 222*, 196.

Hitch, G.J., & Baddeley, A.D. (1976). Verbal reasoning and working memory. *Quarterly Journal of Experimental Psychology, 28*, 603–621.

Johnson-Laird, P.N. (1983). *Mental models*. Cambridge: Cambridge University Press.

Johnson-Laird, P.N., & Bara, B. (1984). Syllogistic inference. *Cognition, 16*, 1–62.

Johnson-Laird, P.N., & Byrne, R. (1991). *Deduction*. Hove: Lawrence Erlbaum Associates Ltd.

Klauer, K.C., Stegmaier, R., & Meiser, T. (1997). Working memory involvement in propositional and spatial reasoning. *Thinking and Reasoning, 3*, 9–48.

Logie, R.H. (1995). *Visuo-spatial working memory*. Hove: Lawrence Erlbaum Associates Ltd.

Meyer, D.E., & Kieras, D.E. (1997). A computational theory of executive cognitive processes and multiple task performance: Part 1. Basic mechanisms. *Psychological Review, 104,* 3–65.

Polk, T.A., & Newell, A. (1995). Deduction as verbal reasoning. *Psychological Review, 102,* 533–566.

Rips, L.J. (1994). *The psychology of proof: Deductive reasoning in human thinking.* Cambridge, MA: MIT Press.

Simon, H.A. (1978). Rationality as process and product of thought. *American Economic Association, 68,* 1–16.

Simon, H.A., & Kaplan, C.A. (1989). Foundations of cognitive science. In M.I. Posner (Ed.), *Foundations of cognitive science* (pp. 1–47). Cambridge, MA: MIT Press.

Stenning, K., & Oberlander, J. (1995). A cognitive theory of graphical and linguistic reasoning: Logic and implementation. *Cognitive Science, 19,* 97–140.

Stevenson, R.J. (in press). Deductive reasoning and the distinction between implicit and explicit processes: A commentary on Evans and Over. *Cahiers de Psychologie Cognitive.*

Sternberg, R.J., & Turner, M.E. (1981). Components of syllogistic reasoning. *Acta Psychologica, 47,* 245–265.

Sutherland, S. (1992). *Irrationality.* London: Penguin Books.

Toms, M., Morris, N., & Ward, D. (1993). Working memory and conditional reasoning. *Quarterly Journal of Experimental Psychology, 46A,* 679–699.

Wetherick, N.E., & Gilhooly, K.J. (1995). "Atmosphere", matching and logic in syllogistic reasoning. *Current Psychology, 14,* 169–178.

Wilkins, M.C. (1928). The effect of changed material on the ability to do formal syllogistic reasoning. *Archives of Psychology, 102,* 5–83.

Woodworth, R.J., & Sells, S.B. (1935). An atmosphere effect in formal syllogistic reasoning. *Journal of Experimental Psychology, 18,* 451–460.

CHAPTER THREE

The Role of Working Memory in Age Differences in Reasoning

Louise H. Phillips
University of Aberdeen, Scotland, UK

Mark J. Forshaw
Coventry University, UK

Since the early part of the century there has been empirical evidence of adult age differences in reasoning (Yerkes, 1921). There is now a rich seam of evidence that increasing age results in poorer performance on some cognitive tasks (those which are relatively effortful, novel, and complex), but not others (those which are relatively automatic, practised, and simple). However, controversy still rages as to the cause of such age deficits. Recent parsimonious theories promote age declines in "working-memory capacity" to explain the poorer performance of older adults on reasoning tasks. In this chapter we will evaluate such theories, by outlining the age differences in working memory and in reasoning, evaluating methodologies used to link the two concepts, and then reviewing the empirical evidence that working memory can explain age differences in reasoning.

AGE DIFFERENCES IN WORKING MEMORY

Although a number of different models of working memory are currently debated (Baddeley & Hitch, 1974; Carpenter, Just, & Shell, 1990; Moscovitch & Winocur, 1992), there is agreement that working memory can be defined as a system for simultaneous retention and manipulation of information. Age-related declines have been reported in a variety of working-memory paradigms. The most common method of assessing "working-memory capacity" is to use a variation on the sentence span task devised by Daneman and Carpenter (1980), with processing such as sentence verification or mental arithmetic. Older adults have lower spans on such tasks (e.g. Norman, Kemper, & Kynette, 1992; Salthouse, 1992a). "Keeping track" tasks are proposed to tap the "memory-updating" facility of working memory (Morris & Jones, 1990). Keeping track of both visuo-spatial and verbal information has been shown to decline with age (Detweiler, Hess, & Ellis, 1996; Dobbs & Rule, 1989). Also, the production of random strings of numbers is thought to depend heavily on the executive processes of working memory (Baddeley, 1986), and older subjects produce less randomly distributed strings than their younger counterparts (Van der Linden, Bregart, & Beerton, 1994).

More controversial is the debate on how best to conceptualise age differences in working memory. Two particular areas of dispute have concerned whether age affects storage or processing aspects of working memory; and whether age differences are best conceptualised in terms of loss of capacity, or executive dysfunction.

By definition, working-memory (WM) tasks must contain both processing and storage elements. Some authors have suggested that age differences in WM are due to a decline in the amount of material that can be stored in memory (Foos, 1989; Parkinson, Inman, & Dannenbaum, 1985). However, others argue that short-term passive storage of material is not much affected by age (Craik & Jennings, 1992; Dobbs & Rule, 1989). Age differences in simple, serial-recall tasks, although reliably found, tend to be fairly small in magnitude compared with the changes found in working-memory tasks (Craik & Jennings, 1992). Craik, Morris, and Gick (1990) found that incrementing memory load did not increase age differences in WM, and concluded that storage differences did not underlie the relationship between WM and age.

A number of authors have proposed that age differences in WM are caused by the inability of older adults to carry out processing operations successfully (Craik et al., 1990; Salthouse, Mitchell, Skovoronek, & Babcock, 1989; Van der Linden et al., 1994). The main method of investigating this hypothesis has been to look for an interaction between age and processing complexity in working-memory tests. However, the results of such manipulations have been mixed, with some studies finding that increased processing complexity differentially impedes the elderly (Craik et al., 1990; Salthouse et al., 1989), whereas others find no interaction between age and processing complexity (Salthouse, Babcock, & Shaw, 1991). In fact, the results obtained seem to depend on the nature of the processing in the working-memory task, and other factors such as the magnitude of complexity variation, the degree of retrieval support and task demands. It may be difficult to separate working-memory tasks into memory and processing components, as both make demands on the same limited capacity resources (Baddeley & Hitch, 1974; Craik & Jennings,

1992). In many WM tasks, individuals must choose how to trade-off the resources devoted to storage with those devoted to processing.

A more contentious issue is whether age differences in WM are best explained in terms of capacity or strategic variation. Baddeley (1986) outlines two ways of conceptualising a measured deficit in WM: either as a dysfunction of executive control functions, or as a reduction in available resource capacity. Much of the ageing literature has concentrated on the latter proposal: that age differences in WM reflect a decrease in the amount of cognitive resources that can be shared out to deal with competing task demands. This maps on to the predominant limited-resource model of working memory in the North American literature.

In relation to the Baddeley and Hitch three-component model of working memory, it has been argued that increased age results in localised decline of the central-executive component, as opposed to the peripheral verbal and visuo-spatial slave systems (Baddeley, 1986), and empirical evidence supports this distinction (Fisk & Warr, 1996). Dysfunction of the central-executive component would be expected to affect high-level aspects of cognition, such as planning, generation of task strategies, monitoring, and error detection and correction. There is neuropsychological evidence to support the idea of age declines in executive function: Age changes in brain volume are most prominent in the frontal lobes (Coffey et al., 1992), which are now known to be involved in executive control processes (Shallice, 1982). Related to the notion of executive control, it has been proposed that increased age results in poorer ability to inhibit irrelevant information (Hasher & Zacks, 1979). This could be especially important in working-memory tasks, where interruptions of rehearsal and processing through attending irrelevant information could result in very poor performance.

Although capacity and executive theories of ageing have very different theoretical implications, in practice, it is often difficult to distinguish between them. For example, the generation of an effective task strategy may demand both effective executive processes and high resource capacity. Indeed, a recent paper argues that reported age differences in central-executive function are attributable to low-level limitations on the speed of processing information (Fisk & Warr, 1996).

So, although age differences in WM are very well documented, what it actually means to have a low "working-memory capacity" is still not clear.

AGE DIFFERENCES IN REASONING

In this chapter, reasoning tasks that have been studied in relation to working memory and age are considered. Some authors specify that only novel tasks can be considered to tap reasoning (Salthouse, 1992b), whereas others include the application of expertise among reasoning tasks (Blanchard-Fields, 1996). Some apparently contradictory findings in this area may be attributable to the assortment of definitions of reasoning used by the various writers and researchers, not to mention the lack of definitions provided by a great many. Perhaps too often, theoretical conclusions about reasoning tasks are dependent on operational definitions of reasoning. Such conclusions therefore rest on properties of the *tasks* themselves rather than on the *psychological processes* underpinning successful performance.

There is ample evidence of age-related deficits in the ability to carry out novel reasoning tasks. The first empirical evidence of such deficits was reported by Yerkes (1921) in relation to the mass US Army intelligence testing of the First World War. Age correlations with tests specifically designed to tap abstract reasoning ability, such as Raven's Matrices (Raven, 1960), average −0.6 (Salthouse, 1993); probably the highest of any replicable correlations between age and cognitive performance. Monotonic linear declines in reasoning ability appear to begin early: from about age 30 onwards (Salthouse, 1991). However, the many confirmations of the relationship between age and reasoning ability have not resulted in any consensus as to its cause. Yerkes argued that age differences in intelligence-test scores reflected changing sampling pressures among different generations of army officers. More recent cross-sequential age studies have led to the conclusion that there are strong generational differences in reasoning ability, as well as genuine developmental changes (Schaie & Parham, 1977). Although the strength of generational changes in reasoning ability is disputed, there is agreement that for many individuals beyond age 65 abstract reasoning ability declines.

However, age differences are not found on all reasoning tasks. Growing older (and, therefore, more experienced) conveys benefits in solving cross-word puzzle clues given some previous experience (Forshaw, 1994), or problem-solving in an occupational setting (Perlmutter, Kaplan, & Nyquist, 1990). Specific expertise and knowledge may partially protect against the effects of ageing. Later in this chapter we will deal in more detail with issues of test novelty and expertise.

METHODOLOGICAL ISSUES IN EXAMINING THE ROLE OF WORKING MEMORY IN AGE DIFFERENCES IN REASONING

Two types of analysis are used to look at the role of working memory in cognition: differential and experimental manipulations. Differential analyses examine hypotheses by first examining overlapping variance between age and cognitive performance (e.g. reasoning), and then statistically manipulating a resource index (e.g. working-memory capacity). Experimental analyses, by contrast, involve direct manipulation of resource requirements (e.g. by incrementing working-memory load).

Differential analyses

Resource hypotheses propose that individuals differ in the amount of fundamental cognitive resources (e.g. WM capacity) available. It is therefore not possible to directly manipulate the main explanatory variable, as WM capacity is proposed to reflect a fundamental limitation on processing. However, statistical techniques can simulate this manipulation: In many studies WM capacity is partialled out of age differences in reasoning (for explanations of the logic of this procedure see Hertzog & Dixon, 1996; Salthouse, 1991). If the partialling procedure results in a reduction in variance overlap between age and reasoning, age differences in reasoning are attributed to reduced WM capacity.

There are problems with the use of statistical control methods that should be borne in mind when interpreting results. The data obtained are correlational, and therefore assumptions about causality must be treated with caution. Also, these partialling techniques assume that the effects of age and working memory are additive and linear, and do not usually test for interactions between age and resource limitations (Hertzog & Dixon, 1996). There are a number of different statistical techniques to look at the reduction in shared variance between age and reasoning ability once memory measures are partialled out, but as yet no established method of testing for the probability that such a reduction occurred owing to chance factors. It is therefore a matter of judgement as to whether a particular magnitude of reduction in variance is meaningful, i.e. "significant".

There is also a fundamental problem with differential techniques: The assumption that "working-memory capacity" is validly assessed by current tests. Because no standardised tests of working memory are available, the validity, sensitivity, and reliability of the different measures used vary considerably. Indeed, there are often poor intercorrelations between different measures of working memory (see, e.g. Gilinsky & Judd, 1994). It is often assumed that these WM measures reflect "cognitive primitives" (Hertzog & Dixon, 1996), i.e. low-level resource limitations, as opposed to higher-level differences such as strategy use. This assumption warrants further investigation, because strategic factors are likely to be important in multi-demand WM tasks. Some of the WM tasks involve fairly complex processing, for example, mental arithmetic (Salthouse & Babcock, 1991), text comprehension (Salthouse & Babcock, 1991), or even sequentially presented deductive reasoning (Kyllonen & Christal, 1990), so that the WM tasks are alarmingly reminiscent of the reasoning tasks that they are supposed to explain. It is indeed circular logic that proposes that differences in tasks of complex reasoning can be explained by variance in tasks of complex reasoning (with an extra memory load) (Kyllonen & Christal, 1990).

Experimental analyses

Various experimental methods of investigating the effect of age differences in working memory on cognition have been reported, including: incrementing the working-memory load in reasoning tasks; adding concurrent tasks to reasoning performance; carrying out probe memory tests for aspects of reasoning performance; and comparing sequential with simultaneous presentation of stimuli. In relation to a "working-memory capacity" theory of ageing, it is predicted that older adults should perform worse under higher WM load conditions. However, concerns have been raised about the interpretation of statistical interaction terms in relation to age (Hertzog & Dixon, 1996; Salthouse, 1991). Experimental studies are often analysed by comparing the effects of a manipulation on extreme age groups, e.g. 20 and 70-year-olds, making such studies particularly susceptible to selection bias and cohort effects. Also, because interactions between age and working memory may be non-linear (e.g. there may be an underlying positively or negatively accelerated interaction between age and increased working memory demands), the presence or absence of an interaction may depend critically on the measurement scale and subsequent transformations used. Finally, such analyses assume that a manipulation can isolate and vary a specific cognitive component, whereas in fact manipulations may qualitatively change the strategies used to attempt tasks, for example, altering position on speed–accuracy trade-off curves (Phillips & Rabbitt, 1995).

REASONING, WORKING MEMORY, AND AGE

Strong claims have been made that *individual differences* in reasoning are highly related to aspects of working memory. For example, Just and Carpenter (1992) propose that language comprehension ability is determined by available WM capacity; and Kyllonen and Christal (1990) argue that all reliable variation in reasoning can be explained by limitations on WM capacity. Following the extensive evidence of WM decline with age, it has frequently been proposed that age differences in reasoning are caused by the limits on WM capacity (e.g. Gilinsky & Judd, 1994; Salthouse, 1993; Zabrucky & Moore, 1995). For the remainder of this chapter, the evidence that age differences in various types of reasoning are attributable to lowered WM capacity will be examined. The reasoning tasks chosen are those on which empirical evidence is available to evaluate the role of working memory in age differences, and are ordered approximately from most novel to most practised: Raven's Progressive Matrices, deductive reasoning, planning, language comprehension, and chess/bridge.

Inductive reasoning: Raven's Progressive Matrices

Probably the strongest age-related deficit on an individual test that has been reported (and replicated countless times) is on Raven's Matrices (RM). Test items involve the presentation of a three-by-three matrix of elements, with the final element left blank (see Fig. 3.1). Subjects analyse the pattern of components to discover underlying rules, and choose the correct answer from multiple options. This test has been used to assess general fluid intelligence for many decades, yet there is still disagreement about the factors underlying differences in performance: whether verbal or spatial, analytic or holistic, culturally determined or culture-free (Richardson, 1991; Roberts & Stevenson, in press). Recent accounts have emphasised the role of working memory in RM performance. Carpenter

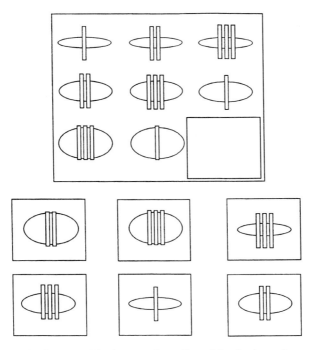

FIG. 3.1   Example of Raven's Matrices type item. One of the six alternatives must be chosen to complete the figure.

et al. (1990) analysed RM performance using eye-tracking and protocol analysis, and concluded that subjects solve RM items by splitting the problem into subgoals in terms of the number of rules to be obeyed. For example, in Fig. 3.1 two rules must be induced regarding: (1) the size of ellipse, and (2) the number of vertical rods. Carpenter et al. (1990) provide evidence that these rules are induced and applied one at a time, and argue that working memory must be heavily involved in RM items in order to work out the rules, and store the results of applying one rule while processing the next.

Various explanations have been put forward to explain the large age deficit in RM performance. It seems likely that some proportion of young–old difference on the task can be explained by the well-documented generational changes in scores (Flynn, 1987; though for counter-arguments see Salthouse, 1991). Also, the role of memory in age differences in RM scores has been highlighted (e.g. Chown, 1961). Two recent studies looked in detail at the role of working memory in age differences in RM.

In a very detailed study using a variety of analyses, Salthouse (1993) found that statistical control of an index of WM capacity accounted for 70% of the age-related variance in RM scores. He concluded that limited ability to preserve information during processing was a major cause of age differences in RM score. However, other analyses did not confirm the involvement of WM in age differences. Increasing the number of rules to be induced per item, and hence presumably the working-memory demands, did not elevate correlations between age and ability to solve items. In fact, increasing the number of rules to be induced in RM items did not elevate correlations with the WM capacity measure, in contrast to Carpenter et al.'s hypothesis that working-memory demands increase when more rules have to be solved. Perhaps the highly selected undergraduate subjects in Carpenter et al.'s study were solving items by serial application of rules (in Hunt's [1974] terms, using an analytic strategy), whereas the more representative (and considerably larger) samples in Salthouse's (1993) study were tackling RM using a qualitatively different (more parallel and holistic) strategy, which did not make such high demands on WM capacity.

Also, Salthouse (1993) found that older subjects had poorer probe-recognition of individual elements of RM items than younger subjects, and were more likely to look repeatedly at particular elements in an item. This might represent the effects of decreased WM capacity. However, WM scores did not predict age differences in number of element inspections. Salthouse also looked at age correlations with separate computerised simultaneous and successive presentations of RM items. In successive presentation items, each of the nine elements of an RM item was presented separately, thus presumably increasing WM demands. However, contrary to working-memory theory, age correlations with RM performance were lower with successive presentation.

Babcock (1994) also found that age differences in RM scores overlapped with variance in WM. In addition, she found that the ability to apply transformation rules to abstract patterns decreased with age, and this explained variance in RM scores independently of the WM capacity measure.

In both the Salthouse (1993) and Babcock (1994) studies, working memory was assessed using solely verbal tests. Given the nonverbal nature of RM items, and the evidence for separation of verbal and visuo-spatial working memory (Farmer, Berman, & Fletcher, 1986; Shah & Miyake, 1996), it is of interest to investigate the role of visuo-spatial working memory in age differences in RM. In a study (Phillips, Gilhooly, Logie, Della Sala, & Wynn, in preparation) involving 60 adults aged from 17 to 75, RM scores were assessed in relation to both verbal and spatial WM. There was, as always, a strong correlation between age and RM (-0.71). However, contrary to the results of Babcock (1994) and Salthouse (1993), statistically removing variance in verbal WM span explained only 3% of the age variation in RM (see Table 3.1). Statistically removing variance due to visuo-spatial WM resulted in a larger attenuation of age–RM variance (19%), but this still leaves the vast majority of overlapping variance to be explained.

These results are in stark contrast to the previously outlined findings. The most likely explanation for this discrepancy is the different tests used to assess working memory. In the Salthouse/Babcock studies, WM capacity was measured by a composite score on tasks of computation span (where

TABLE 3.1
Shared variance (r^2) between age, working memory (WM), Raven's Matrices (RM) and Tower of London (TOL) performance. Figures in rows four and five indicate shared variance between age and reasoning with WM variance partialled out

| | Reasoning index | | |
	RM score	TOL accuracy	TOL speed
r^2 verbal WM	0.029	0.002	0.036
r^2 visuo-spatial WM	0.270	0.109	0.176
r^2 age	0.504	0.096	0.518
remaining r^2 age, verbal WM partialled out	0.489	0.081	0.504
remaining r^2 age, visuo-spatial WM partialled out	0.407	0.040	0.436

a series of arithmetic problems was heard and subjects had to solve each one while retaining the final digit of each problem) and listening span (where a series of sentences was heard, and subjects had to answer a comprehension question on each while retaining the final word of each sentence). Combining the two different measures may be problematic, because correlations between these tasks vary so widely in different studies: from 0.17 (Jurden, 1995) to 0.68 (Salthouse & Babcock, 1991). Jurden also found that computation and listening span differed considerably in the predictions they made of RM scores.

Problems can also be raised with the use of these tasks as measures of low-level resources. Our work with similar tasks has found that subjects are often confused as to which words or digits they are supposed to be recalling. Indeed, Salthouse and Babcock (1991) report that the majority of subjects aged over 70 obtained spans of zero or one on computation and listening span. Does it make sense to think of someone as having a WM capacity of zero? Such scores could indicate a failure to understand task instructions (Gould, 1981). Attaining such low scores on a test of working memory suggests lack of comprehension or compliance with the task demands (relatively high-level cognitive functions), rather than indicating an amount of available low-level cognitive resources. In the Phillips et al. (in preparation) study verbal WM was assessed using a "verification span" task based on one reported by Baddeley, Logie, Nimmo-Smith, and Brereton (1985). The task required true/false judgements on a series of sentences, while remembering the final word from each. The visuo-spatial WM task required estimation of the distance between boxes presented on a computer screen, and simultaneous storage of the location of the boxes. All subjects achieved a span of at least two on the tasks, suggesting that they were able to comply with basic task instructions.

These constrasting findings highlight the difficulty in assessing the role of WM in age differences in reasoning, when (1) no standard measures of working-memory capacity are available; (2) WM tests used often intercorrelate poorly, and (3) the cause of poor performance on the WM tests themselves is poorly understood. The contradictory results, even within Salthouse's 1993 paper, suggest that we need better understanding of the methodological problems before the role of WM in age differences in Raven's Matrices can be evaluated.

Deduction: syllogistic and relational reasoning

Deductive reasoning tasks require the integration of premises (e.g. all B are A, some B are C) in order to reach or evaluate a conclusion (e.g. some A are C). A number of studies have examined the role of working memory in age differences in deductive reasoning. Light, Zelinski, and

Moore (1982) found that older adults were less able than young adults to integrate information across several premises. Salthouse (1992c) examined age differences in relational reasoning, e.g.

> R and S do the OPPOSITE.
> Q and R do the SAME.
> If Q INCREASES, what will happen to S?

Three methods were used: (1) statistical control of working memory; (2) statistical control of a measure of probed memory for task elements; (3) interactions between age and memory load of the syllogisms. Statistical control of a composite measure of computation and listening span reduced by 50% the shared variance between age and reasoning. Also, removing variance due to probe memory reduced substantially the variance overlap between age and reasoning. However, size of working-memory load did not interact with age.

Gilinsky and Judd (1994) also examined age differences in a variety of syllogistic reasoning tasks in relation to working memory. For concrete syllogisms, e.g.

> If all mothers are female,
> and all parents are mothers,
> then all parents are female,

the magnitude of age differences in evaluation was determined by the degree to which the conclusion fitted into prior belief systems (some parents are male . . .) rather than the logic of the syllogism. Belief bias in syllogisms has been well documented (Evans, 1989), and Gilinsky and Judd found that older subjects were more likely than young to accept believable but invalid conclusions. Hierarchical regression analyses revealed that variance in working memory partially explained age differences in syllogistic reasoning. However, reduced WM capacity could not explain the age differences in belief bias.

Cognitive control processes: planning

A recent influential theory of cognitive ageing proposes that changes in the frontal lobes of the brain with age are responsible for cognitive decline (e.g. Moscovitch & Wincour, 1992; Parkin & Walter, 1992). Because this brain area is associated with the operation of cognitive-control functions, such as planning and inhibition of irrelevant material, there is now growing interest in the relationship between age and the control processes of cognitive function. A number of studies show age-related deficits on tasks that require the generation and execution of efficient plans, such as the Tower of Hanoi, or Tower of London (Charness, 1987; Phillips et al., 1996),

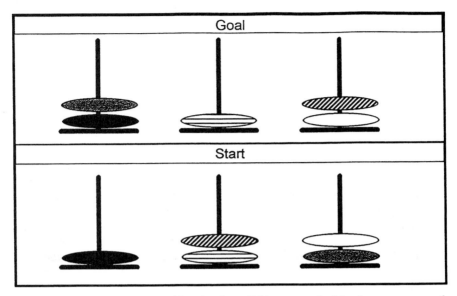

FIG. 3.2   Example of a Tower of London item. Subjects are asked to plan a sequence of moves to transform the "start" to the "goal" state.

for example, see Fig. 3.2. In the Tower of London (TOL) task, subjects must move disks one at a time, until a "start" configuration of disks matches a specified "goal" configuration. The instructions for this task require the full pre-planning of the whole sequence of moves before actually carrying them out.

The TOL should therefore make extensive demands on working memory, because efficient generation and execution of a plan requires simultaneous storage and processing of a number of subgoals. In a recent study (Phillips et al., in preparation, subjects and WM tasks as described in the section on Raven's Matrices) the relationship between age and TOL performance was assessed in relation to verbal and visuo-spatial working memory, results reported in Table 3.1. Age correlated weakly with TOL accuracy, in terms of the number of items solved in the minimum possible moves. Age correlations were much stronger with the speed at which plans were executed. In order to investigate whether age differences in the TOL task were attributable to variation in working memory, verbal and visuo-spatial WM measures were partialled from TOL performance indicators, and remaining shared variance with age examined (Table 3.1). The analysis suggests that the major source of age differences in the TOL, time to execute plans, was not attributable to reduced WM capacity. Support for this comes from the finding that increasing the memory load in the TOL task did not increase the age deficit.

A well-practised task: language comprehension

Language use is possibly the most practised skill in human social existence. It ought, therefore, to be a skill that is not susceptible to age-related changes in working memory. However, prose is often written in such a way that one must *interpret* what has been said. The comprehension of metaphorical constructions, for instance, represents a reasoning task in itself, because one must deal with such figurative language in a special way, "working out" what is meant. For example, when reading the sentence "*He was nothing but a worn-out van chugging away up a cruel hill*", most readers will realise that the subject of the sentence is not really a four-wheeled vehicle and the hill has no intention of being cruel. But in the process of comprehension a leap was made, however quickly and effortlessly, from the literal to the abstract, recreating the intended meaning. The literal information must be stored temporarily while it is checked against contextually appropriate concepts. The processing of such language seems relatively automatic, and so should not heavily load working memory. But, it can be difficult to uncover the meaning behind certain pieces of highly figurative discourse, such as poetry, and there is a process of conscious, controlled, effortful reasoning going on when we attempt this.

An extensive literature documents age declines in processing linguistic information. The main recent focus of such literature has been on the role of working memory in age differences in comprehending texts (see, e.g. chapters in Light & Burke, 1988). Just and Carpenter (1992) have proposed a "capacity theory of comprehension", focusing on the limitations that working memory capacity places on understanding complex texts. They predict that age differences in text processing will occur only when syntactic constructions have high working-memory demands. Norman et al. (1992) found that only some types of syntactic complexity resulted in age differences in comprehension. Older subjects were well able to comprehend texts rich in multiclause sentences, but age differences in comprehension did emerge on texts with many "left-branching" sentences (e.g."*The police whom everyone distrusted were controlled by the mayor*"). Age differences in text comprehension for passages high in left-branching sentences were partially explained by variation in working-memory capacity. Reading speed was also important: older adults were considerably slower at reading left-branching sentences. Across a whole passage, this suggests that working-memory capacity and reading speed may interact; those with low WM capacity would read more slowly, but would also have to retain information presented early in the text for *longer* than those who read quickly. Thus slower reading speed in older adults (Norman et al., 1992) would place even higher demands on already limited WM resources.

Recent evidence supports the idea that WM limitations may only be important when information to be integrated is separated in time. Zelinski (1988) found that older adults can successfully integrate new facts with information from an immediately previous sentence (anaphoric reference), even when the sentence structure places relatively high demands on WM. Tompkins, Bloise, Timko, and Baumgaertner (1994) also found that there was no association between WM and linguistic task performance in normally ageing subjects, although there was in brain-damaged elderly participants. In order to understand anaphora, the reader must hold in WM key aspects of the previous material, usually the subject and object of each sentence. Occasionally a verb may be substituted by a generic verb such as *to do*, as in: "*He flew all around the world. Years later, he did it again.*" The separation of original sentence from the anaphoric one causes problems for any reader, regardless of age, if the distance is too great. Indeed, the maximum acceptable distance is part-and-parcel of the pragmatic rules that any language develops. For older adults with limited WM, the maximum distance may be shorter. Brebion, Ehrlich, and Tardieu (1995) found no age difference in detecting incongruity, if the words suggesting inconsistency were only one word apart, e.g. "*Tales lead us to inflatable lands where animals talk to children*"; whereas there was a significant age difference in detecting incongruity if the inconsistent words were further spaced, e.g. "*The sparrow-hawk can circle for hours without diving at its chair*". In addition, Zabrucky and Moore (1995) found that there was no age difference in detecting inconsistencies when information was presented in adjacent sentences. However, if the inconsistent statements were further apart, age differences did emerge.

There is also evidence to suggest that some WM and language deficits associated with ageing might be attributable to intrusion errors. Arbuckle and Gold (1993) looked specifically at verbosity (irrelevant or inconcise speech) in older people and found that it could be explained by measures of inability to suppress inappropriate information in WM. This suggests an executive, attentional control deficit rather than a capacity or speed-of-processing change. Similarly, Zabrucky and Moore (1995) found that older adults made more personal elaborations of text passages (e.g. "I find news very trite and uninteresting") at recall than did younger adults. The quantity of personal elaborations related to WM-capacity measures, suggesting that age differences in both comprehension and working-memory capacity tests may be influenced by the extent to which older adults fail to inhibit irrelevant information.

Tasks involving expertise: chess and bridge

Although most studies have concentrated on age differences in novel reasoning performance, a number of investigators have instead focused on age differences in tasks requiring expertise. A problem, however, can arise in making the distinction between novel and non-novel tasks. To begin with, what task can be said to be truly novel in its entirety? For example, as most tasks in the literature involve language at some stage in their execution, feeding into and from a non-novel system is essential. Then, of course, one can have no control over the strategies used by the experimental subjects who tackle our laboratory problems. Even when given, for instance, a visuo-spatial task designed to minimise the involvement of language processes, some subjects will "translate" the problem into workable linguistic framework (e.g. Daigneault & Braun, 1993), and draw parallels between the novel aspect of the task and previous experience.

Likewise, it is difficult to speak of tasks as wholly non-novel, as even the most practised of skills will have novel components in their execution. We should, more correctly, speak of a continuum of familiarity, with the utterly familiar at one end and the utterly unfamiliar at the other, while accepting that the two extremes are, in reality, unattainable. Many practised skills fall somewhere in the middle of this continuum, and they are what Glaser and Chi (1988) call "open" skills, because there is always a degree of unpredictability inherent in their execution. Driving is an open skill, as one can never know what lies around the corner in an unfamiliar area or what other drivers will do that you will have to react to. For these skills, the ratio of heuristics to algorithms is greater than for "closed" ones. The contribution of working memory to the execution of open skills will be greater than that for closed skills, as more application and processing of the givens is necessary to achieve the goal state.

Chess is one example of an open skill that has been extensively researched. Charness (1981) found that, among expert chess players, skill levels predicted performance on chess-related tasks (e.g. choosing which move to make next, classifying endgames as win, lose, or draw). However, age did not predict performance on these tasks. By contrast, older experts had poorer memory for chess-related information. A similar pattern was found in relation to bridge playing: No age differences were found amongst expert bridge players for performance on bridge-related tasks, yet older experts again had poorer memory for relevant information. This suggests that in expert domains, older individuals still experience decreases of working-memory capacity. However, they may be able to compensate for this decrease by applying particularly efficient strategies acquired through experience. Bosman and Charness (1996) conclude that ageing involves an interaction between declining WM resources and increasing expertise, which will result in poor performance on novel tasks, but adequate performance on skill-related tasks.

At least one study also provides tentative evidence that expertise in old age is associated with better performance on tasks outside the domain of expertise. Clarkson-Smith and Hartley (1990) found that older experts in bridge performed better on a task of working-memory capacity than age-matched non-experts. This evidence could be interpreted to suggest that regular practice at a specific cognitive task, such as bridge, protects individuals from age-related decline. On the other hand, individuals more inclined to become bridge experts might already be selected for high WM capacity. Some evidence contrary to the latter position is that the experts and non-experts did not differ in terms of vocabulary scores or reaction times, as might be expected if the experts were generally more elite.

CONCLUSIONS

When information must be preserved during active and effortful processing, working-memory limitations may be important in ageing. Although there are no age differences in the *rate* of decay of information (Salthouse & Babcock, 1991), older adults encode, rehearse, and process less information in unit time; therefore, any complex cognitive activity requiring a combination of these processes will take longer, allowing more opportunity for information encoded early in the task to decay. Salthouse (1992a) provides evidence that most of the age differences in working memory can be statistically explained by variation in speed of processing.

The evidence that WM underlies age differences in reasoning is more equivocal than might be expected, given the widespread assumption of the importance of working memory. Finding support for the role of WM in cognitive ageing seems to depend on both the type of task examined and the method used to address WM differences. When analyses are carried out by statistical manipulation, measures of WM capacity often explain age differences in cognitive performance. However, this seems to depend crucially on the task used to assess WM: widely varying amounts of age variance in Raven's Matrices were explained by different WM tasks. Because there are no standardised measures available, questions can be raised about the validity of individual WM tasks.

When experimental manipulations (e.g. of working-memory load) are carried out, the role of WM in age differences depends on the type of cognitive task investigated. Tasks that depend heavily on acquired skill or knowledge (e.g. expert chess performance) are not affected by age declines in working-memory capacity. By contrast, tasks which demand on-line processing and simultaneous preservation of information over time (e.g.

comprehension of texts with complex syntactic structure) are more susceptible to age declines in working memory.

This leaves a puzzle: Why are age differences in apparently novel tasks such as Raven's Matrices, deductive reasoning, and the Tower of London not exacerbated by increases in working-memory load? One explanation is that although ideal performance on these tasks demands cognitive processes with high working-memory load (i.e. inducing and applying rules in RM, deductive reasoning in syllogisms, and pre-planning in the TOL), subjects do not tend to carry out the desired processes. In response to an effortful cognitive task, most individuals attempt to reduce the load by adapting or developing less resource-demanding strategies (Belmont, Freeseman, & Mitchell, 1988). In relation to reasoning tasks, strategies may be used that reduce the demand simultaneously to process and to preserve information across time. This would suggest that many reasoning tasks may involve adapted domain-specific retrieval strategies from what Ericsson and Kintsch (1995) call *long-term working memory*, rather than the limited-capacity short-term working memory of the Baddeley and Hitch model.

For example, in RM, although select undergraduates use analytic WM-demanding strategies (Carpenter et al., 1990), a more representative sample of people might tend to rely on more holistic strategies, which do not increment WM demands when more rules are involved in accurate solution. In syllogistic reasoning, most subjects tend to adopt "matching" or "atmosphere" strategies that are not as accurate as true deduction, but make fewer demands on working-memory resources (Gilhooly, Logie, Wetherick, & Wynn, 1993). The evidence of Gilinsky and Judd (1994) that older subjects are more biased by prior belief when evaluating syllogisms suggests that they are not solving the items in a method that places heavy demands on WM. Finally, in the TOL task, most subjects seem to avoid the high working-memory load of planning an entire sequence of moves, and instead focus only on a few moves at a time. "Working memory" may indeed be a useful concept in cognitive psychology, but subjects taking part in cognitive tests find ingenious ways to avoid loading their own limited-capacity workspace.

This review necessarily concentrates on verbal processes, because so few ageing studies concern non-verbal tasks. It is of interest to speculate on the role of working memory in age differences in visuo-spatial cognition. Age differences have been noted in tasks such as mental rotation, route-finding, etc., though there has been little investigation of the role of visuo-spatial working memory in relation to age differences in these tasks. As outlined above, age changes in verbal working memory are inextricably linked to the rate at which information is processed. Visuo-spatial encoding, rehearsal, and processing mechanisms are less well understood, but may be more holistic and less serial in nature than verbal equivalents. They may therefore be less susceptible to age-related changes in processing speed. This may mean that age differences in visuo-spatial working memory are qualitatively different in nature from those in verbal WM.

The question of whether age differences in reasoning tasks are attributable to working memory remains unresolved. The involvement of working memory may depend on: (1) the cognitive demands of the reasoning task, in particular, whether it can be attempted using practised strategies, and also whether it requires the maintenance of new information during active processing; and (2) the method used: whether experimental or correlational. It is often assumed that working-memory limitations must affect older adults' performance on reasoning tasks, but this depends on experimental participants' solving the reasoning tasks using the conscious, effortful processes hoped for by the experimenter.

ACKNOWLEDGEMENTS

The experimental work reported in this chapter was funded by a grant from the Economic and Social Research Council to Louise Phillips, Ken Gilhooly, Robert Logie, and Sergio Della Sala. The experiments were carried out by Val Wynn.

REFERENCES

Arbuckle, T.Y., & Gold, D.P. (1993). Ageing, inhibition, and verbosity. *Journals of Gerontology, 48*, 225–232.

Babcock, R.L. (1994). Analysis of adult age differences on the Raven's Advanced Progressive Matrices test. *Psychology and Aging, 9*, 303–314.

Baddeley, A.D. (1986). *Working memory*. Oxford: Oxford University Press.

Baddeley, A.D., & Hitch, G. (1974). Working memory. In G.A. Bower (Ed.), *Recent advances in learning and motivation* (Vol. 8, pp. 647–667). New York: Academic Press.

Baddeley, A.D., Logie, R.H., Nimmo-Smith, I., & Brereton, N. (1985). Components of fluent reading. *Journal of Memory and Language, 24*, 119–131.

Belmont, J.M., Freeseman, L.J., & Mitchell, D.W. (1988). Memory as problem solving: the cases of young and elderly adults. In M.M. Gruneberg, P.E. Morris, & R.N. Sykes (Eds.), *Practical aspects of memory: current research and issues* (pp. 84–89). Chichester: Wiley.

Blanchard-Fields, F. (1996). Social cognitive development in adulthood and ageing. In F. Blanchard-Fields, & T.M. Hess (Eds.), *Perspectives on cognitive change in adulthood and aging* (pp. 454–487). New York: McGraw-Hill.

Bosman, E.A., & Charness, N. (1996). Age-related differences in skilled performance and skill acquisition. In F. Blanchard-Fields, & T.M. Hess (Eds.), *Perspectives on cognitive change in adulthood and aging* (pp. 428–453). New York: McGraw-Hill.

Brebion, G., Ehrlich, M.-F., & Tardieu, H. (1995). Working memory in older subjects: dealing with ongoing and stored information in language comprehension. *Psychological Research, 58*, 225–232.

Carpenter, P.A., Just, M.A., & Shell, P. (1990). What one intelligence test measures: a theoretical account of processing in the Raven Progressive Matrices task. *Psychological Review, 97*, 404–431.

Charness, N. (1981). Search in chess: age and skill differences. *Journal of Experimental Psychology: General, 110*, 21–38.

Charness, N. (1987). Component processes in bridge bidding and novel problem-solving tasks. *Canadian Journal of Psychology, 41*, 223–243.

Chown, S.M. (1961). Age and the rigidities. *Journal of Gerontology, 16*, 353–362.

Clarkson-Smith, L., & Hartley, A.A. (1990). The game of bridge as an exercise in working memory and reasoning. *Journal of Gerontology: Psychological Sciences, 45*, 233–238.

Coffey, C.E., Wilkinson, W.E., Parashos, I.A., Soady, S.A.R., Sullivan, R.J., Patterson, I.J., Figiel, G.SA, Webb, M.C., Spritzer, C.E., & Djang, W.T. (1992). Quantitative cerebral anatomy of the ageing human brain: a cross-sectional study using magnetic resonance imaging. *Neurology, 42*, 527–536.

Craik, F.I.M., & Jennings, J.M. (1992). Human Memory. In F.I.M. Craik, & T.A. Salthouse (Eds.), *The Handbook of Aging and Cognition* (pp. 51–110). Hillsdale, NJ: Lawrence Erlbaum Associates Inc.

Craik, F.I.M., Morris, R.G., & Gick, M.L. (1990). Adult age differences in working memory. In G. Vallar, & T. Shallice (Eds.), *Neuropsychological impairments of short-term memory* (pp. 247–267). New York: Cambridge University Press.

Daigneault, S., & Braun, C.M.J. (1993). Working memory and the self-ordered pointing task: further evidence of early prefrontal decline in normal ageing. *Journal of Clinical and Experimental Neuropsychology, 15*, 881–895.

Daneman, M., & Carpenter, P.A. (1980). Individual differences in working memory and reading. *Journal of Verbal Learning and Verbal Behaviour, 19*, 450–466.

Detweiler, M.C., Hess, S.M., & Ellis, R.D. (1996) The effects of display layout on keeping track of visual-spatial information. In W.A. Rogers, A.D. Fisk, & N. Walker (Eds.), *Aging and skilled performance* (pp. 157–184). Hillsdale, NJ: Lawrence Erlbaum Associates Inc.

Dobbs, A.R., & Rule, B.G. (1989). Adult age differences in working memory. *Psychology and Aging, 4*, 500–503.

Ericsson, K.A., & Kintsch, W. (1995). Long-term working memory. *Psychological Review, 102*, 211–245.

Evans, J.St.B.T. (1989). *Bias in human reasoning.* Hillsdale, NJ: Lawrence Erlbaum Associates Inc.

Farmer, E.W., Berman, J.V.F., & Fletcher, Y.L. (1986). Evidence for a visuo-spatial scratch-pad in working memory. *Quarterly Journal of Experimental Psychology, 38*, 675–688.

Fisk, J.E., & Warr, P. (1996). Age and working memory: the role of perceptual speed, the central executive, and the phonological loop. *Psychology and Aging, 11*, 316–323.

Flynn, J.R. (1987). Massive IQ gains in 14 nations: What IQ tests really measure. *Psychological Bulletin, 101*, 171–191.

Foos, P.W. (1989). Adult age differences in working memory. *Psychology & Aging, 4*, 269–275.

Forshaw, M.J. (1994). *Expertise and ageing: the crossword puzzle paradigm.* Unpublished doctoral dissertation, University of Manchester.

Gilhooly, K.J., Logie, R.H., Wetherick, N.E., & Wynn, V. (1993). Working memory and strategies in syllogistic reasoning tasks. *Memory and Cognition, 21*, 115–124.

Gilinsky, A.S., & Judd, B.B. (1994). Working memory and bias in reasoning across the lifespan. *Psychology and Aging, 9*, 356–371.

Glaser, R., & Chi, M.T.H. (1988). Overview. In M.T.H. Chi, R. Glaser, & M.J. Farr (Eds.), *The nature of expertise* (pp. 1–18). Hillsdale, NJ: Lawrence Erlbaum Associates Inc.

Gould, S.J. (1981). *The mismeasure of man.* London: Penguin.

Hasher, L., & Zacks, R.T. (1979). Automatic and effortful processes in memory. *Journal of Experimental Psychology: General, 108*, 356–388.

Hertzog, C., & Dixon, R.A. (1996). Methodological issues in research on cognition and ageing. In F. Blanchard-Fields, & T.M. Hess (Eds.), *Perspectives on cognitive change in adulthood and old age* (pp. 66–121). New York: McGraw-Hill.

Hunt, E.B. (1974). Quoth the Raven? Nevermore! In L.W. Gregg (Ed.), *Knowledge and Cognition* (pp. 129–158). Hillsdale, NJ: Lawrence Erlbaum Associates Inc.

Jurden, F.H. (1995). Individual differences in working memory and complex cognition. *Journal of Educational Psychology*, 87, 93–102.

Just, M.A., & Carpenter, P.A. (1992). A capacity theory of comprehension: Individual differences in working memory. *Psychological Review*, 99, 122–149.

Kyllonen, P.C., & Christal, R.E. (1990). Reasoning ability is (little more than) working memory capacity. *Intelligence*, 14, 389–433.

Light, L.L., & Burke, D.M. (Eds.). (1988). *Language, memory and aging*. Cambridge: Cambridge University Press.

Light, L.L., Zelinski, E.M., & Moore, M.M. (1982). Adult age differences in reasoning from new information. *Journal of Experimental Psychology: Learning, Memory and Cognition*, 8, 435–447.

Morris, N., & Jones, D.M. (1990). Memory updating in working memory: The role of the central executive. *British Journal of Psychology*, 81, 111–121.

Moscovitch, M., & Winocur, G. (1992). The neuropsychology of memory and ageing. In F.I.M. Craik, & T.A. Salthouse (Eds.), *The handbook of aging and cognition* (pp. 315–372). Hillsdale, NJ: Lawrence Erlbaum Associates Inc.

Norman, S., Kemper, S., & Kynette, D. (1992). Adult reading comprehension: Effects of syntactic complexity and working memory. *Journal of Gerontology: Psychological Sciences*, 47, 258–265.

Parkin, A.J., & Walter, B.M. (1992). Recollective experience, normal ageing and frontal dysfunction. *Psychology and Aging*, 7, 290–298.

Parkinson, S.R., Inman, V.W., & Dannenbaum, S.E. (1985). Adult age differences in short term forgetting. *Acta Psychologica*, 60, 83–101.

Perlmutter, M., Kaplan, M., & Nyquist, L. (1990). Development of adaptive competence in adulthood. *Human Development*, 33, 185–197.

Phillips, L.H., Gilhooly, K.J., Logie, R.H., Della Sala, S., & Wynn, V. (1996). *The role of memory in the Tower of London task*. Paper presented at the Second International Conference on Memory, Abano (PD), Italy.

Phillips, L.H., Gilhooly, K.J., Logie, R.H., Della Sala, S., & Wynn, V. (in preparation). Age, memory and planning.

Phillips, L.H., & Rabbitt, P.M.A. (1995). Impulsivity and speed–accuracy strategies in intelligence test performance. *Intelligence*, 21, 13–29.

Raven, J.C. (1960). *Guide to the Standard Progressive Matrices*. London: H.K. Lewis.

Richardson, K. (1991). Reasoning with Raven—in and out of context. *British Journal of Psychology*, 61, 129–138.

Roberts, M.J., & Stevenson, N.J. (in press). Reasoning with Raven: with and without help. *British Journal of Psychology*.

Salthouse, T.A. (1991). *Theoretical perspectives on cognitive aging*. Hillsdale, NJ: Lawrence Erlbaum Associates Inc.

Salthouse, T.A. (1992a). Influences of processing speed on adult age differences in working memory. *Acta Psychologica*, 79, 155–170.

Salthouse, T.A. (1992b). Reasoning and spatial abilities. In F.I.M. Craik, & T.A. Salthouse (Eds.), *The handbook of aging and cognition* (pp. 167–211). Hillsdale, NJ: Lawrence Erlbaum Associates Inc.

Salthouse, T.A. (1992c). Working-memory mediation of adult age differences in integrative reasoning. *Memory and Cognition*, 20, 413–423.

Salthouse, T.A. (1993). Influence of working memory on adult age differences in matrix reasoning. *British Journal of Psychology, 84,* 171–199.

Salthouse, T.A., & Babcock, R.L. (1991). Decomposing adult age differences in working memory. *Developmental Psychology, 27,* 763–776.

Salthouse, T.A., Babcock, R.L., & Shaw, R.J. (1991). Effects of adult age on structural and processing capacities in working memory. *Psychology and Aging, 6,* 118–127.

Salthouse, T.A., Mitchell, D.R.D., Skovoronek, E., & Babcock, R.L. (1989). Effects of adult age and working memory on reasoning and spatial abilities. *Journal of Experimental Psychology: Learning Memory and Cognition, 15,* 507–516.

Schaie, K.W., & Parham, I.A. (1977). Cohort-sequential analyses of adult intellectual development. *Development Psychology, 13,* 649–653.

Shah, P., & Miyake, A. (1996). The separability of working memory resources for spatial thinking and language processing: An individual differences approach. *Journal of Experimental Psychology, 125,* 4–27.

Shallice, T. (1982). Specific impairments of planning. *Philosophical Transactions of the Royal Society of London. B, 298,* 199–209.

Tompkins, C.A., Bloise, C.G.R., Timko, M.L., & Baumgaertner, A. (1994). Working memory and inference revision in brain-damaged and normally ageing adults. *Journal of Speech and Hearing and Speech Research, 37,* 896–912.

Van der Linden, M., Bregart, S., & Beerton, A. (1994) Age related differences in updating working memory. *British Journal of Psychology, 84,* 145–152.

Yerkes, R.M. (1921). Psychological examining in the United States Army. *Memoirs of the National Academy of Sciences, 15,* 1–877.

Zabrucky, K., & Moore, D. (1995). Elaborations in adults' text recall: Relations to working memory and text recall. *Experimental Aging Research, 21,* 143–158.

Zelinski, E.M. (1988). Integrating information from discourse. Do older adults show deficits? In L.L. Light, & D.M. Burke (Eds.), *Language, memory and aging* (pp. 117–132). Cambridge: Cambridge University Press.

CHAPTER FOUR

Dualism Down the Drain: Thinking in the Brain

Sergio Della Sala and Robert H. Logie
University of Aberdeen, Scotland, UK

THE PHILOSOPHER WHO LOST HIS THOUGHTS

I was a medical student in Jena and attended the lectures and clinic of the famous psychiatrist Professor Otto Binswanger. One day—it must have been in January 1889—a patient who had recently been brought in was led into the classroom. Binswanger presented him to us ... Professor Nietzsche! ... [He] did not at first sight have the external appearance of a sick man ... Sometimes one saw him quiet and friendly, sometimes ... he was in a highly excited state, and his consciousness was apparently troubled ... Nietzsche's case must have been a luetic infection of the brain. (Simchowitz, 1925)

Friedrich Nietzsche (see Fig. 4.1) was one of the great thinkers and philosophers of the nineteenth century. He died at the end of August 1900, after 10 years of an incapacitating brain disease. Various biographies and movie scripts (e.g. *Beyond good and evil*, 1977, by L. Cavani) have suggested that the disease was probably a cerebral syphilis that Nietzsche had contracted some 20 years before (e.g. Moebius, 1902). The slowly progressive cerebral luetic infection hampered his ability for coherent thinking, and relatives and friends could not distinguish his behaviour from that of a madman. However, as is apparent from the numerous reports of the witnesses (see the biographies by Gilman, 1987; Hayman, 1995; Kaufmann, 1974), Nietzsche retained his memory, at least partially. He could speak without any slurring, remained free from movement dis-

45

FIG. 4.1 Detail from Hans Olde's charcoal sketch of Nietzsche in the final stages of his brain disease. Reproduced with permission from *Nietzsche: A critical life* by Ronald Hayman, 1980, London: Phoenix House Publishers.

orders and, until the very end, maintained the appearance of a healthy person.

It is now well known (e.g. Harriman, 1984, p. 258) that neurosyphilis entails very severe and widespread neuronal disruption in the anterior cortex of the brain, the so-called frontal lobes. It appears therefore that Nietzsche suffered from a "frontal" syndrome, and various hints to support this claim can be gleaned from the copious collection of letters from his relatives and friends. His main symptoms are described below along with classic or recent references to other case studies and group studies that have associated such abnormal behaviour with lesions in the frontal lobes (see Fig. 4.2).

Oscillation in behaviour was one of the main features of Nietzsche's brain disease, and occasionally he became boisterous and riotous (Zacher, 1901). He also tended to confuse mental events with external events, and he was convinced that nothing was beyond his powers (Malloy & Duffy, 1994), to the point of believing that he could control events with his thoughts. His friends noticed highly exaggerated humorous antics and a

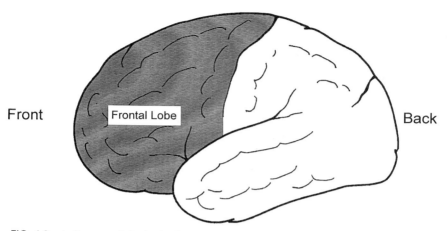

FIG. 4.2   A diagram of the brain showing the site and relative size of the frontal lobes.

tendency to make jokes that were entirely inappropriate (a symptom known as Oppenheim's *Witzelsucht*, 1889). There was often a laughing expression on his face, which his acquaintances believed did not become him (Brickner, 1936). He would often remain silent for most of the day (Luria's dynamic aphasia, 1973), examining favourite objects he had accumulated in five purses (collector's behaviour, Eslinger & Damasio, 1985), with childish excitement (Jastowitz's *moria*, 1888). Occasionally, he would talk continuously and to no apparent purpose, wandering from one subject to another, until he had exhausted himself (Benson's verbal dysdecorum, quoted by Trimble, 1990). Sometimes he wanted to shake hands with anybody he met in the street, even complete strangers (Lhermitte's environmental dependency syndrome, 1986). He had been an accomplished pianist and although he still tried to play the piano, he had lost his sense of rhythm (Leonard, Milner, & Jones, 1988). His reading comprehension was very poor (Rylander, 1939) because he read compulsively individual lines of text (Assal, 1985). His appetite was good, although he never asked for food or drink. He was completely apathetic ("pseudodepression", Blumer & Benson, 1975), had lost his initiative (Kleist's *Antriebmangel*, 1934), and showed a remarkable lack of concern (Campbell, 1909), as if he were no longer experiencing any emotion, neither happiness nor sadness. And, of course, most important to our theme, his streams of thought were often incoherent, and he failed to show hints of cogent reasoning; so much so that one of his friends visiting him in November 1897 pondered "what thoughts might still be alive behind [his] impenetrable external mask" (von Schirnhofer, 1969, p. 449).

By contrast, he recognised his visitors without difficulty, showing an absence of prosopagnosia, although sometimes he perseverated (Luria, 1973) in gestures and actions such as offering his hand repeatedly in greeting. When asked, usually he could supply some basic facts (Shimamura, Janowsky, & Squire, 1991), demonstrating that his semantic knowledge was relatively unimpaired (Janowsky, Shimamura, Kritchevsky, & Squire, 1989), although he would do so acting as a schoolboy who had been forced to do so. Moreover, he did not show overt amnesia (Hécaen & Albert, 1978) and was, at least in the early stages of his disease, well articulated, although he used to speak in a whisper (Damasio & Van Hösen, 1983). He also did not have perceptual deficits and showed pleasure in listening to music. All in all, Nietzsche was not "himself" any more (Harlow, 1868).

This case report illustrates clearly the dramatic influence that brain pathology can have on what were once apparently normal thinking patterns and overt behaviour. Moreover, the substantial literature published subsequently, some of which we have already referenced, suggests that such disorders of thinking can arise from lesions in the frontal lobes. Wilder Penfield, the famous Canadian neurosurgeon, observed (Penfield & Evans, 1935) that the best way to express the effects on his own sister of the excision of a large area of her right frontal lobe affected by a tumour was to say that "she could not think well enough" (p. 131). Despite the accumulating evidence for links between the frontal lobes and thinking and executive functions, the exact nature of these links is still one of the unsolved riddles (Teuber, 1964) of modern cognitive sciences (Darling, Della Sala, Gray, & Trivelli, in press; Rabbitt, in press).

THINKING AS EXECUTIVE FUNCTION

Despite the debate as to the function of the frontal lobes in cognition, it should be clear from the foregoing discussion that a study of the effects of various forms of brain damage may shed light on the link between brain structure and aspects of thinking. It is widely recognised that studying neuropsychological patients in the context of theories of normal cognition has contributed to the understanding of normal memory, language, object recognition, and a range of other cognitive functions. Moreover, these studies have offered significant insight into the nature of the cognitive deficits arising from different forms of brain damage. Likewise, a systematic neuropsychology of thinking may advance theories of normal thinking, and these theories in turn can contribute to the interpretation of neuropsychological deficits.

As is apparent from most of the chapters in this book, thinking in its broadest sense incorporates putative higher cognitive functions, to include planning, problem-solving, reasoning, and decision-making. Although this is not necessarily a comprehensive list, there is some debate as to which other forms of cognitive activity ought to be included. For example, it would be difficult to consider thinking without the support of prior knowledge such as fluency in language or expertise in a particular domain (e.g., Ericsson & Kintsch, 1995). Within the domain of neuropsychology, only some of the various cognitive processes mentioned so far have been studied in any depth, and those that have been studied are often referred to as executive functions (for a review, see Tranel, Anderson, & Benton, 1994). The concept of thinking as such rarely arises. Indeed, there are cognitive processes that are subsumed under the heading of executive functions that might not traditionally be considered part of human thinking, for example, dual-task co-ordination (for a review, see Della Sala & Logie, 1993) or the allocation of attention (for a review, see Stuss, Eskes, & Foster, 1994), or the initiation of cognitive activity and self-monitoring (e.g., Lezak, 1995). Indeed, Benson (1994, p. 260) has stated that executive control should not be considered synonymous with thinking. We are sympathetic to this view, but would argue that there is considerable overlap, with the cognitive functions of thinking relying on a subset of executive functions. It is this "thinking subset" of executive functions that will be the focus of this chapter, but, as will become clear, there are some of the "thinking" executive functions, such as reasoning, for which the published neuropsychology literature is scant, whereas other areas, such as planning and problem-solving, have been the subject of extensive study. It is these latter areas that offer a corpus of data for a neuropsychology of thinking. We will draw on these data to discuss the nature of the cognitive architecture that might be involved in such tasks, and shall conclude by suggesting ways in which the neuropsychology of thinking might fruitfully be developed.

NEUROLOGICAL BASIS OF THINKING

In most textbooks of neuropsychology there are no specific chapters on thinking. When thinking is mentioned it is either not given any special status (e.g. Lezak, 1995) or is regarded "a function of the entire brain that defies localization" (Glonig & Hoff, 1969), or is dealt with only in part with chapters on planning or problem-solving (Das, Kar, & Parrila, 1996, chapter 4; McCarthy & Warrington, 1990, chapter 16; Young, 1978, chapter 17). Current views of brain function assume a significant degree of modularity, and this assumption is supported by a range of neuropsychological double dissociations (Shallice, 1988). It may be, therefore, that the frontal lobes support only some executive functions, with thinking being an emergent property of several modules acting in concert. However, the science of human cognitive neuropsychology comprises not only the mapping of cognitive function on to neurological function, but also the understanding of the functional organisation of the brain. As such, it incorporates not only neuroanatomical mapping of cognitive functions, but also links between cognitive functions and electrical and biochemical activity in the brain. It also includes the development of theoretical models of normal cognitive functions derived at least in part from studies of brain-damaged patients. The major approach has been to undertake extensive studies of patients who have suffered brain damage. However, there is now a growing literature on the neurological activity of the normal brain in cognitive tasks. This was driven initially by the observation of changes in brain electrical activity when subjects were asked simply to "think" (e.g. Chapman, 1973), and more recently by various brain-imaging techniques such as Positron Emission Tomography (PET) (e.g., D'Esposito, Deter, Alsop, Shin, Atlas, & Grossman, 1995; Nichelli, Grafman, Pietrini, Alway, Carton, & Miletich, 1994).

The approach to a cognitive neuropsychology of executive functions has followed a path similar to that for other areas of cognitive neuropsychology, although its history has been somewhat sporadic, and concrete theoretical development has been rather elusive. As mentioned earlier, a common conclusion from studies of patients with impairment of executive functions has been that their deficits arise from damage to the frontal lobes. However, this link in itself is not very informative, not least because the frontal lobes comprise a substantial area of the brain (more than 30%, Fuster, 1989). Thinking, clearly, is a complex process, which may well involve several forms of brain function acting together. If we accept that thought processes are the result of the interaction between complex and different neuronal networks, the obvious consequence is that several neurological disorders can affect thinking. Indeed, deficits in thinking have been observed not only in patients with localised lesions in the frontal lobes due to stroke or tumour, but also in patients who have brain damage resulting from very different aetiologies, such as head injury, schizophrenia (Gray, 1981), Alzheimer's disease (Della Sala, Logie, & Spinnler, 1992). Table 4.1 lists neurological diseases that can give rise to disorders of executive function (dysexecutive syndrome, Baddeley & Wilson, 1988; Tranel et al., 1994). It is beyond the purpose of this chapter to describe these disorders in any detail and the interested reader is referred to dedicated monographs (e.g. Benson, 1994) or clinical neurology textbooks (e.g. Adams & Victor, 1989).

Deficits in performance on tests of thinking (as already defined) have also been found in patients with focal lesions in more posterior areas of the brain (Glosser & Goodglass, 1990; Tranel et al., 1994). Finally, it is a strong and widespread assumption when interpreting task impairments in patients that the site of their damage is also the area of the brain that is

TABLE 4.1
Common diseases of the central nervous system that can affect the cognitive
function of thinking

Intracranial neoplasms (especially frontal tumours or metastasis)
Degenerative diseases (e.g. dementia of the Alzheimer's type)
Psychiatric disorders (e.g. schizophrenia)
Some viral (e.g. herpes encephalitis), pyogenic (e.g. anterior brain abscess) and other non-viral infection (e.g. neurosyphilis)
Cerebrovascular diseases (e.g. frontal stroke)
Head injury (very frequent frontal lesions)
Some demyelinative disease (e.g. multiple sclerosis)
Acquired metabolic disorders (e.g. hypothyroidism)
Inherited metabolic diseases (e.g. intermittent porphyria)
Nutritional deficiency (e.g. Wernicke-Korsakov syndrome)
Disorders due to chemical agents (e.g. lead poisoning) or alcohol (alcoholism)

necessarily used in the healthy brain for performance of the same tasks (e.g. Farah, 1994). It is possible, for example, that the impaired performance reflects the operation of intact areas of the brain that have been employed by the patients to perform tasks that would normally involve the damaged area. However, although such alternative intact areas may accomplish the tasks, they may do so less efficiently or in a radically different fashion from the damaged areas that were responsible for task performance prior to the injury. For all these reasons, we feel it is more useful to focus on deficits in the performance of executive functions rather than link the deficits specifically with frontal-lobe damage. As a result, we will argue for a more theoretically based approach, that incorporates operational definitions of impaired function. In so doing, we will consider the range of paradigms that have been used to study those cognitive functions we have defined under the general heading of "human thinking", and will attempt to explore potential theoretical pathways towards an architecture for the cognitive system(s) that might be responsible. Before embarking on a discussion of the contemporary literature, we shall set the historical context in which a neuropsychology of thinking has developed.

HISTORICAL BACKGROUND OF A NEUROPSYCHOLOGY OF THINKING

The idea of a link between the brain and cognition can be traced back to the ancient Egyptian physicians and Greek philosophers (Changeux, 1985). For example, both Plato (Taylor, 1929) and Hippocrates (Adams, 1849) viewed the brain as the seat of thought. Even Aristotle, who objected to the cephalocentric thesis, nevertheless supported the existence of internal thought, maintaining for instance, that "when one thinks of something large that is not currently present, one necessarily does so by mental activity"[1] (Ross, 1955, chapter 2, 452b, 10–11). The idea of an organ of thought became very unpopular for the following two millennia largely as a result of it being too materialist a view for the political and religious *Zeitgeist*. Liu Zhi (1704, quoted by Zhu, 1989), a Chinese scholar at the beginning of the eighteenth century, listed "thinking" as one of the five "internal perceptions" of the brain, although he localised it "in the middle part of the brain". Thomas Reid, a former Professor of Philosophy at the University of Aberdeen, identified six intellectual powers of the mind (Reid, 1785/1969), namely, memory, conception, abstraction, judgement, reasoning, and taste (i.e. aesthetics); but he did not propose any links with parts of the brain. It was only with the phrenologists (Gall, 1798; Spurzheim, 1815) that some faculties of the mind, such as judgement (*Vergleichendersinn*) and reasoning (*Folgerungsvermögen*), were assigned to the most anterior areas of the brain (see Fig. 4.3), "usually in the 'organ' right below the rim of the hair" (Canziani, 1838). Often, the work of Gall

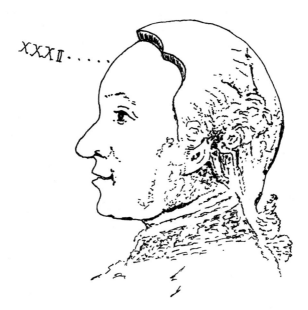

FIG. 4.3 Portrait of Immanuel Kant reproduced by Spurzheim (1815) as evidence that a prominent frontal area was characteristic of persons predisposed to reasoning and thinking. This portrait, which is from 1786, is now at the "Archiv für Kunst und Geschichte" in Berlin.

---

[1] This is our translation from the Ross (1995) edition. The original Greek text was: "νοει γαρ τα μεγαλα και πορρω ου τω αποτεινειν εκει την διανοιαν ωσπερ την οψιν φασι τινες (και γαρ μη οντων ομοιως νοησει) αλλα τη αναλογον κινησει."

and Spurzheim is described as a rather simplistic mapping of various personality characteristics and abilities to the contours of the skull. However, their early work, which is less well known, was based on observations of brain structures, and it was only later that they turned to popularising the mapping of "bumps on the head". Specifically, following detailed post-mortem examinations of a number of brains, Gall and Spurzheim were among the first researchers to postulate links between localised brain damage and specific cognitive or personality deficits.

By the middle of the nineteenth century there was wide acceptance of the brain as being an organ of thought, and that variations between the personality and abilities of individuals were linked to differences in brain structure or that "Men judge things according to the organisation of their brain" (Spinoza, 1843). However, it was not until the famous case of Phineas Gage (Harlow, 1848, 1868) that there was clear evidence of "systems in the human brain dedicated more to reasoning than to anything else" (Damasio, 1994, p. 10). Gage was a 25-year-old railway construction foreman, whose skull was penetrated by a tamping iron when an explosive charge detonated prematurely. The rod, which was 1 m long and 3 cm in diameter, entered just below his left cheek and emerged through the top of his skull on the right side. The lesion spared all of the posterior areas of the brain but inflicted considerable bilateral damage to the frontal lobes. Considerable detail about the injury was obtained when Gage's exhumed skull was examined by means of modern neuroimaging techniques (Damasio, Grabowski, Frank, Galaburda, & Damasio, 1994). The most astonishing feature of this case was that Gage apparently suffered no cognitive deficits, but there was a profound change in his personality, coupled with a lack of any sense of responsibility or acknowledgement of social norms of behaviour, and an inability to implement plans. The changes were so dramatic that those who had known him before his accident commented that "he was no longer Gage" (Harlow, 1868, p. 340). He found it extremely difficult to retain regular employment because the "change in his mind [was] so marked that they could not give him his place again" (Harlow, 1868, p. 339), and he ended up working as a "freak" for the Barnum circus (Cahill, 1983). Similar cases have been reported in the literature more recently, showing a clear dissociation between personality and cognitive functions (Brazzelli, Colombo, Della Sala, & Spinnler, 1994; Eslinger & Damasio, 1985; Shallice & Burgess, 1991). Cases like these suggest that damage to the frontal lobes is associated with a lack of ability to inhibit spontaneous behaviour. These kinds of changes that follow frontal lobe damage were interpreted as early as 1876 by Ferrier as "a form of mental degradation which may be reduced . . . to the loss of the faculty of attention' (p. 288).

For many years, the precise function of the frontal lobes was a mystery.

Although damage to many other areas of the brain (e.g. Broca's and Wernicke's areas) had long been known to have dramatic, well-documented, and consistent consequences, the frontal lobes appeared to be able to sustain considerable damage without any clearly defined effects upon reasoning, memory, or other cognitive functions. For example, those who have sustained extensive damage to their frontal lobes may continue to score well on standardised intelligence tests (Hebb & Penfield, 1940; Warrington, James, & Maciejewski, 1986).

In the 1960s, discoveries such as those by Milner and her associates (Milner, 1963; 1964) held out some hope that it would be possible to identify regions in the frontal lobes that controlled such functions as language, memory, problem-solving, and reasoning. When the search for such loci failed to bear fruit, however, that early optimism began to wane. At the same time, a variety of changes of a more diffuse nature have been reported in frontal patients (Luria, 1973). These more nebulous effects of frontal damage are many and multifarious. For example, there have been numerous reports of personality changes (Feuchtwanger, 1923; Harlow, 1848; 1868; Jastrowitz, 1888; Oppenheim, 1889; Penfield & Evans, 1935); impaired ability for abstract thinking (Goldstein, 1927; 1944); impaired initiative and verbal ideation (Kleist, 1934); difficulty in synthesising cognitive operations (Brickner, 1936), distractability (Ackerly, 1937; Ackerly & Benton, 1948; Fuster, 1989; Hécaen & Albert, 1978); defects of selective attention (Hécaen & Albert, 1978; Nauta, 1964; Scheibel, 1981; Skinner & Yingling, 1977) and of sustained attention (Fuster, 1980; Lezak, 1995; Luria, 1966; Stuss & Benson, 1986); diminished alertness (Benson & Geschwind, 1975; Hécaen, 1964; Plum & Posner, 1980); impaired verbal fluency (Risse, Rubens, & Jordan, 1984; Smith & Milner, 1984; Incisa della Rochetta, 1986; Jetter, Poser, Freeman, & Markowitsch, 1986; Janowsky et al., 1989); and impaired planning ability (Shallice, 1982).

Over the past 10 years, on the basis of these and other findings, many researchers have concluded that, rather than performing specific cognitive or linguistic functions, the frontal lobes are more concerned with the organisation and deployment of these resources. In other words, the frontal lobes have come to be regarded as having a controlling or "executive" function, an umbrella term denoting abilities such as planning, mental productivity, decision-making, abstract reasoning, judgement, and behavioural monitoring and modulation. The behavioural and cognitive deficits shown by frontal patients have commonly been attributed to an impairment of executive functioning, which is believed to be the special province of this region of the brain; in fact, as Tranel et al. (1994) have pointed out, the terms "frontal" and "executive" are used interchangeably by many authors. However, more recent developments in the understanding of the executive functions have shown that they do not map exclusively on to functioning of the frontal lobes. This has been shown in healthy adults with PET studies (see review in Foster, Black, Buck, & Bronskill, in press). Moreover, the so-called "frontal tests" are sensitive to damage in different areas of the brain as well as in the pre-frontal cortex (e.g. Anderson, Damasio, Jones, & Tranel, 1991; Reitan & Wolfson, 1994; Robbins, James, Owen, Sahakian, McInnes, & Rabbitt, in press). It seems fair to maintain that different parts of the brain interact throughout the process of thinking. These certainly include the frontal lobes, but need the collaboration of perception from the posterior cortex, the associations provided by anatomical and biochemical links between brain structures, the "spur" from the "emotional" limbic system and the "satisfactions of achievement that are linked with the life promoting activities of the hypothalamus and the reticular system" (Young, 1978, p. 204). Therefore, labelling a set of deficits as comprising a "frontal syndrome" offers little for the development of theories of normal cognition or for the understanding of the nature of the cognitive deficits from which some individuals suffer following damage to their brain.

COGNITIVE MODELS OF EXECUTIVE FUNCTION

A few theoretical frameworks have been developed to account for very specific aspects of thinking such as mental arithmetic (McCloskey, Harley, & Sokol, 1991) or language processing (Just & Carpenter, 1992). These models cannot account for most of the neuropsychological data described so far. However, there are a number of contemporary theoretical models of cognition that might offer a platform for interpreting a range of executive dysfunctions. These models are not entirely incompatible although they vary in detail and in the range of functions for which they are designed to account. Moreover, the models were not originally devised as frameworks for the study of executive function, but rather to account for temporary or working memory (Baddeley, 1986), or for the development and use of expertise (Ericsson & Kintsch, 1995) or for the control of action and the causes of "action slips" (Norman & Shallice, 1986).

Despite the initial motivation for their development, these models have offered cogent accounts for some aspects of executive function and dysfunction as already defined. For example, the concept of working memory incorporates a central-executive component, which appears to have a role in co-ordinating cognitive performance in multiple tasks in healthy adults (e.g. Logie, Zucco, & Baddeley, 1990). This co-ordination function has been shown to be specifically impaired in Alzheimer's patients, and this impairment has been interpreted as reflecting a deficit in the central executive of working memory (Baddeley, Bressi, Della Sala, Logie, & Spinnler, 1991; Baddeley, Logie, Bressi, Della Sala, & Spinnler, 1986). A similar interpretation has been offered to account for dual-task co-ordination deficits in other neurological disorders such as Parkinson's disease (Dalrymple-Alford, Kalders, Jones, & Watson, 1994) and traumatic brain injury (Hartman, Pickering, & Wilson, 1992). Moreover, recent studies have reported a link between behavioural disorders and impairments of dual-task co-ordination in patients with frontal-lobe damage (Alderman, 1996; Baddeley, Della Sala, Papagno, & Spinnler, 1997; Cowey & Green, 1996).

A more detailed model of the central executive has been derived from the Norman and Shallice (1986; Shallice & Burgess, 1996) "supervisory attentional system" (SAS). This model has been used successfully in accounting for slips of action in normal subjects (Norman & Shallice, 1986). Dysfunction of the SAS has been postulated to account for deficits in control of action such as in frontal patients showing "utilisation behaviour" (Brazzelli, Colombo, Della Sala, & Spinnler, 1994; Shallice, Burgess, Schon, & Baxter, 1989), a syndrome in which actions that are driven by external stimuli cannot be inhibited. Other studies of frontal-lobe patients have used a similar interpretation to account for deficits in divided attention (Godefroy & Rousseaux, 1996) and in controlling shifts of attention such as in the widely used Wisconsin Card Sorting Task (Milner, 1963; for a review, see Stuss et al., 1994). However, deficits on these tasks are not unique to frontal-lobe damage, with similar impairments observed in patients with posterior lesions (e.g., Anderson et al., 1991; for a critical review, see Reitan & Wolfson, 1994). Moreover, in studies of healthy adults, performance on the Wisconsin Card Sorting Task has been shown to be dependent on the operation of the phonological-loop component of working memory rather than simply on shifts of attention (Dunbar & Sussman, 1995).

A deficit of the SAS also has been implicated in disorders of planning (Shallice, 1982) and of divided attention shown by patients with frontal-lobe damage. For example, Shallice and Burgess (1991) described three head-injured patients with damage to the pre-frontal cortex who had particular difficulties in everyday tasks that involved formation of strategies for effective performance. In one task, the patients were asked to buy a series of simple everyday items from different shops, to find out details such as the price of tomatoes or the rate of exchange for the French Franc, and then to arrange to be at a meeting point at a particular time. All three patients made more errors on this task than did a group of nine control subjects, for example, entering the same shop more than once or leaving a shop without paying for goods. Shallice has also reported poor performance in patients with frontal-lobe damage on a novel problem-solving task known as the "Tower of London" (Owen, Downes, Sahakian, Polkey, & Robbins, 1990; Shallice, 1982; 1988). On the whole, these results have been replicated, although some doubt has been cast on their interpretation. For instance, Goel and Grafman (1995) tested 20 patients with lesions in the pre-frontal cortex with the Tower of Hanoi (an earlier version of the Tower of London). In all cases, performance was impaired relative to controls; however, Goel and Grafman conclude that the failure of the patients could not be attributed to failures of planning moves in the task. It appeared more likely that poor performance resulted from failures of short-term memory or in resolving conflicts between goals and subgoals when progressing towards a solution. Recent studies in our own laboratory have shown that in the Tower of London task, healthy adults appear not to rely on the executive function of "planning" thought to be subsumed within the SAS (see chapter by Phillips and Forshaw in this volume).

TOWARDS A COGNITIVE ARCHITECTURE OF "THE THINKER"

The SAS model, then, may offer a means by which to understand some of the deficits observed in tasks that rely on control of attention or planning of actions. However, the equivocal nature of the tasks employed thus far highlights the need to undertake detailed cognitive task analysis before performance patterns can be attributed to any of the executive functions. This limitation of the current literature becomes even more acute when attempting to map executive functions on to neuroanatomical structures. The paradigms of the cognitive psychology of thinking, such as think-aloud protocols (Ericsson & Simon, 1984) or dual-task methodologies (Gilhooly, Logie, Wetherick, & Wynn, 1993) can offer alternative approaches to the systematic analyses of tasks used in assessment of patients with dysexecutive symptoms. The application of such paradigms in studies of brain-damaged patients could in turn facilitate the further development of a neuropsychology of thinking.

We argued earlier that some executive dysfunctions can be understood within specific and coherent cognitive models. Might this approach be used to provide accounts of deficits in other aspects of thinking that may be observed in neuropsychological patients? One clear example of a key area of normal thinking, not considered in the neuropsychological literature, is that of reasoning. There is a substantial body of published research on reasoning in healthy subjects (see, e.g., Gilhooly, 1996 for a review), and recent studies have examined whether working memory might provide a theoretical framework for the cognitive processes involved in reasoning tasks (Gilhooly et al., 1993; see Chapters 2 and 3 in this volume). In experimental studies, Gilhooly et al. have demonstrated that normal subjects will commonly avoid heavily loading executive functions when performing reasoning tasks, if they can achieve acceptable levels of performance using less cognitively demanding strategies. Healthy subjects will, however, use strategies equivalent to formal logical rules when trained or specifically instructed to do so. Therefore, should a patient be suspected of having a deficit in reasoning ability, it would be crucial to consider their performance levels in the context of the normal tendency to "satisfice" rather than achieve high levels of performance, that is, to comply with task demands while avoiding effortful cognition.

One feature of both the working-memory model and the SAS model is the notion of a central controlling system, which could be likened to an homunculus. An immediate reaction to this concept is that it simply leads to an infinite regress, with the homunculus being controlled by some other "higher-order" homunculus and so on, thereby risking theoretical sterility. One resolution is to view the homunculus as a system comprising several different but interrelated processes such as in the SAS model (Shallice & Burgess, 1996). This offers a rather complex framework, but one that, despite its limitations, has been shown to have utility in dealing with neuropsychological data. Alternatively, Baddeley (1986; Baddeley and Della Sala, 1996) has argued that the homunculus offers a theoretical holding device, serving as a means to wrap up the executive functions within a general conceptual framework, while the accumulation of data allows its gradual fractionation. Neuropsychological data, in particular, point to dissociations that assist the process of fractionation (Brazzelli et al., 1994; Eslinger & Damasio, 1985; Shallice & Burgess, 1991). This approach has the attraction that some limited and well-defined sets of observed phenomena can be accounted for by those aspects of a theoretical framework that have been well specified. These more limited "sub-theories" make testable predictions leading to further development and application. The remaining phenomena, which cannot be accounted for by the well-developed "sub-theories" can be left to other theories that deal specifically with those phenomena or, in the case of what we have referred to as the executive functions, they are parcelled up into the homunculus until such time as theories allow these phenomena to be dealt with more adequately. This theoretical device is not unique to any one particular cognitive framework, but clearly has considerable heuristic value, and makes the executive phenomena more tractable. The concern then about the possibility of an infinite regress is more apparent than real unless the hierarchy of homunculi is seen as a permanent feature of the theory.

In the early part of this chapter, we raised the issue of the ambiguity surrounding the concept of thinking within neuropsychology. It should be clear from our discussion that there appears to be a partial overlap between the executive functions studied in neuropsychological patients and those cognitive functions that might be incorporated in a neuropsychology of thinking. Thinking also relies on other "non-executive" cognitive functions. For example, thinking skills can be acquired (see, e.g. Gilhooly, 1996), and the way in which subjects perform a given task may depend crucially on their knowledge bases and available heuristics in the relevant domains. Therefore, it may be the nature of prior knowledge and expertise that provides insight into thinking rather than the assumed cognitive demands of the task in hand (Ericsson & Kintsch, 1995; see Chapter 6 in this volume by Ericsson & Delaney).

This possible variability in acquired knowledge between individuals has important implications for some of the techniques in neuropsychology. For example, the neuropsychological double dissociation (e.g. Shallice, 1988) is a powerful technique for aiding the theoretical fractionation of cognitive functions. However, in the case of thinking, double dissociations may arise from differences in the pre-traumatic knowledge bases of the patients concerned. This in turn emphasises the need to carry out a detailed analysis of the task demands so as to be clear as to the nature of the assumed background knowledge in the subject as well as the nature of the on-line cognitive functions necessary for adequate task performance.

Therefore, thinking can be considered to arise from a range of cognitive functions acting in concert and drawing on stored knowledge. A breakdown in any of these functions can hamper thinking ability. Impairments of thinking could also arise from a breakdown in the link between past experience and on-line cognition. Indeed, this form of breakdown has been proposed to account for the disorders of thinking associated with schizophrenia (Gray, 1991). In developing a neuropsychology of thinking, the approach of postulating subtheories offers considerable scope, with each subtheory addressing particular aspects of thinking and their possible patterns of breakdown. This leaves us with the problem of mapping thinking processes on to neuroanatomy. The evidence we have discussed so far demonstrates that damage to the frontal lobes is associated with impairments in some executive functions. However, these executive functions on their own cannot be equated with thinking. A functional view of thinking is as the operation of several cognitive functions in collaboration with stored knowledge, so too any form of neuroanatomical mapping must allow for the operation of several different brain structures and networks acting together. Indeed, it has been suggested that the frontal lobes might act as the locus where all sensorial information converges with subjective knowledge and personal emotions (Gardner, 1993, p. 263).

There is a very long history of debate as to whether it is possible to specify the nature of the link between the brain and the mind. In a large part, progress was hampered, until the late nineteenth century, by the influence of the religious establishment in western Europe. However, even after there was widespread acceptance that thinking and other mental experience arose from the functioning of the brain, the pessimism about resolving the mind–body problem persisted, for example, in the writings of Stout[2] (1898). Borrowing an illustration from McDougall (1911, p. 352), Stout (1921, 3rd Edn) commented

> Even if the brain of a man could be so enlarged that all the members of an International Congress of Physiologists could walk about inside his nerve fibres and hold a conference in one of his "ganglion cells", their united knowledge and the resources of all their laboratories could not suffice to enable them to discover a feeling or sensation or perception or idea... (p. 16).

One might argue that the recent development of neuroimaging techniques and theoretical modelling allow figurative implementation of the brain enlargement referred to by Stout. Notwithstanding the recent advances in neuroscience and in connectionist modelling, we are still a long way from solving the mind–body problem. Indeed, recently Jacobson (1993) stated that "Exactly how mental phenomena may emerge from physical processes has never been explained" (p. 120). One possible route to a resolution is to suggest that the cognitive function of the brain simply offers a different level of explanation from that offered by neurophysiology. Thinking then arises as an emergent property of the way in which the neurophysiology operates, thereby hinting at a refutation of Descartes' dualism (Eaton, 1927). However, given the different levels of explanation, an examination of neurophysiology cannot help much in accounting for intact and impaired thinking. In particular, the short-hand term "frontal deficit" begs too many questions, whereas the cognitive concept of dysexecutive functioning offers a basis for the correct level of explanation necessary for a neuropsychology of thinking.

The main focus of this volume is on the relationship between working memory and thinking. An approach based on cognitive neuropsychology rather than neurophysiology or neuroanatomical mapping has done much to develop the concept of working memory and the phonological and visuo-spatial subcomponents (Baddeley, 1996; Della Sala & Logie, 1993; Logie, 1995). Although a well-specified theory of the executive component(s) of working memory and its dysfunction remains a goal rather than an achievement, clearly the route to that goal is beginning to benefit significantly from this functional approach.

---

[2] G.F. Stout established the Department of Psychology at the University of Aberdeen, Scotland, in 1896. The first edition of his "Manual of Psychology' was published in 1898.

ACKNOWLEDGEMENTS

We thank Dr Jonathan Friday for his help in gleaning some of the sources of Nietzsche's biography. We are also grateful to the University of Bergen for providing office and library facilities during the preparation of this manuscript.

REFERENCES

Ackerly, S. (1937). Instinctive, emotional and mental changes following prefrontal lobe extirpation. *American Journal of Psychiatry, 92*, 717–729.

Ackerly, S.S, & Benton, A.L. (1948). Report of case of bilateral frontal lobe defect. *Research Publication of the Association Nervous & Mental Disorders, 27*, 479–504.

Adams, F. (1849). *The genuine books of Hippocrates*. London: Sydenham Society.

Adams, R.D., & Victor, M. (1989). *Principles of neurology* 4th Edn. New York: McGraw-Hill.

Alderman, N. (1966). Central executive deficit and response to operant conditioning methods. *Neuropsychological Rehabilitation, 6*, 161–186.

Anderson, S.W., Damasio, H., Jones, R.D., & Tranel, D. (1991). Wisconsin card sorting test as a measure of frontal lobe damage. *Journal of Clinical and Experimental Neuropsychology, 13*, 909–922.

Aristotle (*c*. 330BC) *The parva naturalia. De memoria et reminiscentia*. Greek text in D. Ross (Ed.). Oxford: Clarendon Press, 1955.

Assal, G. (1985). Un aspect du comportement d'utilisation: la dependence vis à vis du language écrit. *Revue Neurologique, 141*, 493–495.

Baddeley, A.D. (1986). *Working memory*. Oxford: Oxford University Press.

Baddeley, A.D. (1996). *Human memory: Theory and practice*. Hove: Psychology Press.

Baddeley, A.D., Bressi, S., Della Sala, S., Logie, R.H., & Spinnler, H. (1991). The decline of working memory in Alzheimer's disease: A longitudinal study. *Brain, 114*, 2521–2542.

Baddeley, A.D., & Della Sala, S. (1996). Working memory and executive control. *Philosophical Transactions of the Royal Society of London B, 351*, 1397–1404.

Baddeley, A.D., Della Sala, S., Papagno, C., & Spinnler, H. (1997). Dual-task performance in dysexecutive and nondysexecutive patients with a frontal lesion. *Neuropsychology, 11*, 187–194.

Baddeley, A.D., Logie, R., Bressi, S., Della Sala, S., & Spinnler, H. (1986). Senile dementia and working memory. *Quarterly Journal of Experimental Psychology, 38A*, 603–618.

Baddeley, A.D., & Wilson, B. (1988). Frontal amnesia and the dysexecutive syndrome. *Brain and Cognition, 7*, 212–230.

Benson, D.F. (1994). *The neurology of thinking*. New York: Oxford University Press.

Benson, D.F., & Geschwind, N. (1975). Psychiatric conditions associated with focal lesions of the central nervous system. In S. Arieta & M Reiser (Eds.), *American handbook of psychiatry: Organic disorders and psychosomatic medicine* (pp. 208–243). New York: Basic Books.

Blumer, D., & Benson, D.F. (1975). Personality changes with frontal and temporal lobe lesions. In D.F. Benson & D. Blumer (Eds.), *Psychiatric aspects of neurological disease*. New York: Grune and Stratton,.

Brazzelli, M., Colombo, N. Della Sala, S., & Spinnler, H. (1994). Spared and impaired cognitive abilities after bilateral frontal damage. *Cortex, 30*, 27–51.

Brickner, R.M. (1936). *The intellectual functions of the frontal lobes: Study based upon observation of a man after partial bilateral frontal lobectomy*. New York: Macmillan.

Cahill, R.E. (1983). *New England's witches and wizards*. Peabody, MA: Chandler Smith.

Campbell, D. (1909). Stoerungen der Merkfaehigkeit und fehlendes Krankheitsgefehl beinem Fall von Stirnhirntumor. *Monatsschrift für Psychiatrie, 26,* 33–41.

Canziani, G. (1838). *Principi elementari di frenologia.* Published MD Thesis, University of Milan.

Changeux, J.-P. (1985). The "Organ of the Soul" from ancient Egypt to the Belle Epoque. Chapter 1 in *Neuronal man: The biology of mind.* New York: Pantheon Books.

Chapman, R.M. (1973). Evoked potentials of the brain related to thinking. In F.J. McGuigan and R.A. Schoonover (Eds.), *The psychophysiology of thinking: The study of covert processes* (pp. 69–108). New York: Academic Press.

Cowey, C.M., & Green, S. (1996). The hippocampus: A "working memory" structure? The effect of hippocampal sclerosis on working memory. *Memory, 4,* 19–30.

Dalrymple-Alford, J.C., Kalders, A.S., Jones, R.D., & Watson, R.W. (1994). A central executive deficit in patients with Parkinson's disease. *Journal of Neurology, Neurosurgery and Psychiatry, 57,* 360–367.

Damasio, A.R. (1994). *Descartes' Error.* New York: G.P. Putnam's Sons.

Damasio, H., Grabowski, T., Frank, R., Galaburda, A., & Damasio, A.R. (1994). The return of Phineas Gage: Clues about the brain from the skull of a famous patient. *Science, 264,* 1102–1105.

Damasio, A.R., & van Hösen, G.W. (1983). Emotional disturbances associated with focal lesions of the limbic frontal lobe. In K.M. Heilman and P. Satz (Eds.) *Neuropsychology of human emotion* (pp. 85–110). New York: Guilford Press.

Darling, S., Della Sala, S., Gray, C., & Trivelli, C. (in press). Putative functions of the prefrontal cortex: Historical perspectives and new horizons. In G. Mazzoni and T.O. Nelson (Eds.), *Metacognition and cognitive neuropsychology.* Hillsdale, NJ: Lawrence Erlbaum Associates.

Das, J.P., Kar, B.C., & Parrila, R.K. (1996). *Cognitive planning: The psychological basis of intelligent behavior.* New Delhi: Sage Publications.

Della Sala, S., & Logie, R.H. (1993). When working memory does not work: The role of working memory in neuropsychology. In F. Boller & H. Spinnler (Eds.), *Handbook of neuropsychology* (Vol. 8, pp. 1–63). Amsterdam: Elsevier Publishers.

Della Sala, S., Logie, R.H., & Spinnler, H. (1992). Is primary memory deficit of Alzheimer patients due to a "central executive" impairment. *Journal of Neurolinguistics, 7,* 325–346.

D'Esposito, M., Deter, J.A., Alsop, D.C., Shin, R.K., Atlas, S., & Grossman, M. (1995). The neural basis of the central executive system of working memory. *Nature, 378,* 279–281.

Dunbar, K., & Sussman, D. (1995). Toward a cognitive account of frontal lobe deficits in normal subjects. In J. Grafman, K.J Holyoak, & F. Boller (Eds.), Structure and functions of the human prefrontal cortex. *Annals of the New York Academy of Sciences, 769,* 289–304.

Eaton, R.M. (Ed.) (1927). *René Descartes—Selections.* New York: Scribner.

Ericsson, K., & Kintsch, W. (1995). Long-term working memory. *Psychological Review, 102,* 211–245.

Ericsson, K.A., & Simon, H. (1984). *Protocol analysis: Verbal reports as data.* Cambridge, MA: MIT Press.

Eslinger, P.J., & Damasio, A.R. (1985). Severe disturbance of higher cognition after bilateral frontal lobe ablabation: Patient EVR. *Neurology, 35,* 1731–1741.

Ferrier, D. (1876). *The functions of the brain.* London: Smith and Elder.

Feuchtwanger, E. (1923). *Die Funktionen des Stirnhirns.* Berlin: Springer.

Foster, J.K., Black, S.E., Buck, B.H., & Bronskill, M.J. (in press). Executive and non-executive functions in normal and pathological ageing: A neuroimaging investigation. In P.M.A. Rabbitt (Ed.), *Methodology of frontal executive functions.* Hove: Psychology Press.

Fuster, J.M. (1989). *The prefrontal cortex* (2nd Edn). New York: Raven Press.

Gall, F.J. (1835). *On the functions of the brain and of each of its parts*, Vols I–VI. (W. Lewis, Trans.). Boston: Marsh, Caper & Lyon. (Original work published 1822–1825.)

Gardner, H. (1993). *Frames of mind* (2nd Edn). London: Fontana Press.

Gilhooly, K.J. (1996). *Thinking: Directed, undirected and creative* (3rd Edn). New York: Academic Press.

Gilhooly, K.J., Logie, R.H., Wetherick, N.E., & Wynn, V. (1993). Working memory and strategies in syllogistic reasoning tasks. *Memory and Cognition, 21*, 115–124.

Gilman, S.L. (1987). *Begegnungen mit Nietzsche*. English translation by D.J. Parent: *Conversations with Nietzsche. A life in the words of his contemporaries*. Oxford: Oxford University Press.

Glonig, D., & Hoff., H. (1969). Cerebral localization of disorders of higher nervous activity. In P.J. Vinken and G.W. Bruyn (Eds.), *Handbook of clinical neurology* (Vol. 3: *Disorders of higher nervous activity*, pp. 22–47). New York: Wiley.

Glosser, G., & Goodglass, H. (1990). Disorders in executive control functions among aphasic and other brain damaged patients. *Journal of Clinical and Experimental Neuropsychology, 12*, 485–501.

Godefroy, O., & Rousseaux, M. (1996). Divided and focused attention in patients with lesion of the prefrontal cortex. *Brain and Cognition, 30*, 155–174.

Goel, V., & Grafman, J. (1995). Are the frontal lobes implicated in "planning" functions? Interpreting data from the Tower of Hanoi. *Neuropsychologia, 33*, 623–642.

Goldstein, K. (1927). Die Lokalisation in der Grosshirnrinde. In A. Berthe (Ed.), *Handbuch der Normalen und Pathologischen Physiologie* (pp. 600–842). Berlin: Springer.

Goldstein, K. (1944). The mental changes due to frontal lobe damage. *Journal of Psychology, 17*, 187–209.

Gray, J.A. (1991). The neuropsychology of schizophrenia (plus commentaries). *Behavioral and Brain Sciences, 14*, 1–84.

Harlow, J.M. (1848). Passage of an iron bar through the head. *Boston Medical and Surgical Journal, 39*, 389–393.

Harlow, J.M. (1868). Recovery from the passage of an iron bar through the head. *Publications of the Massachusetts Medical Society, 2*, 327–347.

Harriman, D.G.F. (1984). Bacterial infections of the central nervous system. In J. Hume Adams, J.A.N. Corsellis, and L.W. Duchen (Eds.), *Greenfield's neuropathology*. London: Edward Arnold.

Hartman, A., Pickering, R.M., & Wilson, B.A. (1992). Is there a central executive deficit after severe head injury? *Clinical Rehabilitation, 6*, 133–140.

Hayman, R. (1980). *Nietzsche: A critical life*. London: Phoenix Giant.

Hebb, D.O., & Penfield, W. (1940). Human behaviour after extensive bilateral removals from the frontal lobes. *Archives of Neurology and Psychiatry, 44*, 421–438.

Hécaen, H. (1964),. Mental symptoms associated with tumours of the frontal lobe. In J.M.Warren & K. Akert (Eds.), *The frontal granular cortex and behaviour* (pp. 335–352). New York: McGraw-Hill.

Hécean, H., & Albert, M.L. (1978). *Human neuropsychology*. New York: Wiley.

Incisa della Rochetta, A. (1986). Classification and recall of pictures after unilateral frontal or temporal lobectomy. *Cortex, 22*, 189–211.

Jacobson, M. (1993). *Foundations of neuroscience*. New York: Plenum Press.

Janowsky, J.S., Shimamura, A.P., Kritchevsky, M., & Squire, L.R. (1989). Cognitive impairment following frontal lobe damage and its relevance to human amnesia. *Behavioural Neuroscience, 103*, 548–560.

Jastrowitz, M. (1888). Beiträge zur Localisation im Grosshirn und über deren praktische Verwerthung. *Deutsche Medizinische Wochenschrift, 14*, 81–83, 108–112, 125–128, 151–153, 172–175, 188–192, 209–211.

Jetter, W., Poser, U., Freeman Jr, R.B., & Markowitsch, H.J. (1986). A verbal long-term memory deficit in frontal lobe damaged patients. *Cortex, 22*, 229–242.

Just, M., & Carpenter, P. (1992). A capacity theory of comprehension: Individual differences in working memory. *Psychological Review, 99*, 122–149.

Kaufmann, W. (1974). *Nietzsche: Philosopher, psychologist, antichrist.* Princeton, NJ: Princeton University Press.

Kleist, K. (1934). *Gehirnpathologie.* Leipzig: Barth.

Leonard, G., Milner, B., & Jones, L. (1988). Performance on unimanual and bimanual tapping task by patients with lesions of the frontal or temporal lobe. *Neuropsychologia, 26*, 79–91.

Lezak, M.D. (1995). *Neuropsychological assessment.* New York: Oxford University Press.

Lhermitte, F. (1986). Human autonomy of the frontal lobes. II. Patient behaviour in complex and social situations: The "environmental dependency syndrome". *Annals of Neurology, 19*, 335–343.

Liu, Zhi (1704). *Tian Fang Xing Li* (thread-bound edition).

Logie, R.H. (1995). *Visuo-spatial working memory.* Hove: Lawrence Erlbaum.

Logie, R.H., Zucco, G., & Baddeley, A.D. (1990). Interference with visual short-term memory. *Acta Psychologica, 75*, 55–74.

Luria, A.R. (1966). *Higher cortical functions in man.* New York: Basic Books.

Luria, A.R. (1973). *The working brain: An introduction to neuropsychology.* New York: Basic Books.

Malloy, P., & Duffy, J. (1994). The frontal lobes in neuropsychiatric disorders. In F. Boller, J. Grafman, and H. Spinnler (Eds.), *Handbook of neuropsychology* (Vol. 9, pp. 203–232). Amsterdam: Elsevier.

McCarthy, R.A., & Warrington, E. (1990). *Cognitive neuropsychology.* San Diego: Academic Press.

McCloskey, M., Harley, W., & Sokol, S. (1991). Models of arithmetic fact retrieval: An evaluation in light of findings from normal and brain damaged subjects. Journal of Experimental Psychology: Learning, Memory, and Cognition, 17, 377–397.

McDougall, W. (1911). *Body and mind.* London: Methuen and Co.

Milner, B. (1963). Effects of different brain lesions on card sorting. *Archives of Neurology, 9*, 90–100.

Milner, B. (1964). Some effects of frontal lobectomy in man. In J.M. Warren & K. Akert (Eds.), *The frontal granular cortex and behaviour* (pp. 313–334). New York: McGraw Hill.

Moebius, P.J. (1902). *Über das Pathologische bei Neitzsche.* Wiesbaden: Bergmann.

Nauta, W.J.H. (1964). Some efferent connections of the prefrontal cortex in the monkey. In J.M. Warren & K. Akert (Eds.), *The frontal granular cortex and behaviour* (pp. 397–409). New York: McGraw-Hill.

Nichelli, P., Grafman, J., Pietrini, P., Alway, D., Carton, J.C., & Miletich, R. (1994). Brain activity in chess playing. *Nature, 369*, 191.

Norman, D., & Shallice, T. (1986). Attention to action: Willed and automatic control of behavior. In R.J. Davidson, G.E. Schwartz, & D.E. Shapiro (Eds.), *Consciousness and self-regulation: Advances in research and theory* (Vol. 4, pp. 1–18). New York: Plenum Press.

Oppenheim, H. (1889). Zur Pathologie der Grosshirngeschwulste. *Archiv für Psychiatrie, 21*, 560–578.

Owen, A.M., Downes, J.J., Sahakian, B.J., Polkey, C.E., & Robbins, T.W. (1990). Planning and spatial working memory following frontal lobe lesions in man. *Neuropsychologia, 28*, 1021–1034.

Penfield, W., & Evans, J. (1935). The frontal lobe in man: A clinical study of maximum removals. *Brain, 58*, 115–133.

Phillips, L., Gilhooly, K.J., Logie, R.H., Della Sala, S., & Wynn, V. (1996). The role of memory in the Tower of London Task. *Abstracts of The Second International Conference on Memory*, Abano (PD), Italy, p. 162.

Plum, F., & Posner, J.B. (1980). *The Diagnosis of Stupor and Coma* (3rd Edn). Philadelphia: F.A. Davies.

Rabbitt, P.M.A. (Ed.) (in press). *Methodology of frontal and executive functions*. Hove: Psychology Press.

Reid, T. (1785). *Essays on the intellectual powers of man*. Reprinted 1969. Cambridge, MA: MIT Press.

Reitan, R.M., & Wolfson, D. (1994). A selective and critical review of neuropsychological deficits and the frontal lobes. *Neuropsychology Review, 4*, 161–198.

Risse, G.L., Rubens, A.B., Jordan, L.S. (1984). Disturbances of long-term memory in aphasic patients: A comparison of anterior and posterior lesions. *Brain, 107*, 605–617.

Robbins, T.W., James, M., Owen, A.M., Sahakian, B.J., McInnes, L., & Rabbitt, P.M.A. (in press). A neural systems approach to the cognitive psychology of ageing: Studies with CANTAB on large samples of the normal elderly population. In P.M.A. Rabbitt (Ed.), *Methodology of frontal executive functions*. Hove: Psychology Press.

Ross, D. (Ed.) (1955). *Aristotle: Parva naturalia: De memoria et reminiscentia*. Oxford: Clarendon Press.

Rylander, G. (1939). Personality changes after operations on the frontal lobes. *Acta Psychiatrica et Neurologica Scandinavica, 20*, Suppl., 3–327.

Scheibel, A.B. (1981). The problem of selective attention: A possible structural substrate. In O. Pompeiano & C. A. Marsan (Eds.), *Brain mechanisms of perceptual awareness and purposeful behavior* (pp. 319–326). New York: Raven Press.

Shallice, T. (1982). Specific impairments of planning. *Philosophical Transactions of the Royal Society of London B, 298*, 199–209.

Shallice, T. (1988). *From neuropsychology to mental structure*. Cambridge: Cambridge University Press.

Shallice, T., & Burgess, P.W. (1991). Deficits in strategy application following frontal lobe damage in men. *Brain, 114*, 727–741.

Shallice, T., & Burgess, P.W. (1996). The domain of supervisory processes and temporal organisation of behaviour. *Philosophical Transactions of the Royal Society of London B, 351*, 1405–1412.

Shallice, T., Burgess, P.W., Schon, F., & Baxter, M.D. (1989). The origin of utilisation behaviour. *Brain, 112*, 1587–1598.

Shimamura, A.P., Janowsky, J.S., & Squire, L.R. (1991). What is the role of frontal lobe damage in memory disorders? In H.S. Levin, H.M. Eisenberg, & A.L. Benton (Eds.), *Frontal lobe function and dysfunction* (pp. 173–198). New York: Oxford University Press.

Simchowitz, S. (1925). Der sieche Dionysoz: Eine persoenliche Erinnerung. Koenische Zeitung, August 29, 1925.

Skinner, J.E., & Yingling, C.D. (1977). Central gating mechanisms that regulate event-related potentials and behavior. *Progress in Clinical Neurophysiology, 1*, 30–69.

Smith, M.L., & Milner, B. (1984). Differential effects of frontal-lobe lesions on cognitive estimation and spatial memory. *Neuropsychologia, 22*, 697–705.

Spinoza, B. de (1843). *Ethique*. Paris: Charpentier.

Spurzheim, J.G. (1815). *The physiognomical system of Drs Gall and Spurzheim: Founded on an anatomical and physiological examination of the nervous system in general, and of the brain in particular; and indicating the dispositions and manifestations of the mind*. London: Baldwing, Cradock and Joy.

Stout, G.F. (1898). *Manual of psychology*. London: Clive, University Correspondence College Press.

Stout, G.F. (1921). *Manual of psychology* (3rd Edn). London: Clive, University Tutorial Press.

Stuss, D.T., & Benson, D.F. (1986). *The frontal lobes* (2nd Edn). New York: Raven Press.

Stuss, D.T., Eskes, G.A., & Foster, J.K. (1994). Experimental neuropsychological studies of frontal lobe functions. In F. Boller & H. Spinnler (Eds.), *Handbook of Neuropsychology* (Vol. 9, pp. 149–185). Amsterdam: Elsevier.

Taylor, A.E. (1929). English translation of Plato's *Timaeus*. London: Methuen.

Teuber, H.L. (1964). Some effects of frontal lobotomy in man. In J.M. Warren and K. Akert (Eds.), *The granular cortex and behaviour* (pp. 410–444). San Francisco: McGraw-Hill.

Tranel, D., Anderson, S.W., & Benton, A. (1994). Development of the concept of "executive function" and its relationship to the frontal lobes. In F. Boller and H. Spinnler (Eds.), *Handbook of neuropsychology* (Vol. 9, pp. 125–148). Amsterdam: Elsevier.

Trimble, M.R. (1990). Psychopathology of frontal lobe syndromes. *Seminars in Neurology, 10*, 287–294.

von Schirnhofer, R. (1969). Friedrich Nietzsche und Resa von Schirnhofer. *Zeitschrift für philosophische Forschung, 22*, 449.

Warrington, E.K., James, M., & Maciejewski, C. (1986). The WAIS as a lateralizing and localizing diagnostic instrument: A study of 656 patients with unilateral cerebral lesions. *Neuropsychologia, 24*, 223–239.

Young, J.Z. (1978). *Programs of the brain*. Oxford: Oxford University Press.

Zacher, O.L. (1901). Über ein Fall von doppelseitigem, symmetrisch gelegenem Erwiechung-sherd im Stirhirn und Neuritis optica. *Neurologische Zentralblatt, 20*, 1074–1083.

Zhu, Y.-X. (1989). Historical contributions of Chinese scholars to the study of the human brain. *Brain and Cognition, 11*, 133–138.

CHAPTER FIVE

Working Memory and Comprehension

Randall W. Engle
Georgia Institute of Technology, USA

Andrew R.A. Conway
University of Illinois, USA

It seems intuitively obvious that the temporary retention of information would be important for complex cognitive behaviour such as listening and reading comprehension. In order to comprehend this chapter you must maintain representations of words, phrases, sentences, etc. However, traditional measures of short-term memory (STM) capacity, such as simple digit span, fail to reveal a strong relationship with measures of comprehension, such as the Verbal Scholastic Aptitude Test (VSAT). Baddeley and Hitch (1974) claimed that the lack of a relationship between STM capacity and complex cognition is due to the fact that STM is a passive storage buffer that is not involved in the processing of information. Instead, they proposed a working-memory (WM) system that is responsible not only for the storage of information, but also for the simultaneous processing of information. Working memory, not short-term memory, is the system that will play a role in complex cognitive behaviour, and working-memory capacity, not short-term memory capacity, is the critical constraint on behaviour.

The question we address in this chapter is where and when working memory and working-memory capacity are important for comprehension. Which processes involve WM, and how are these processes constrained by WM capacity? In the case of reading and listening comprehension, the answer is complex. There is clearly a relationship between measures of WM capacity and complex measures of comprehension, such as the VSAT, but why does this relationship occur? Which specific reading processes require WM resources and which do not? Furthermore, what does a WM task measure that is also reflected in complex tests of comprehension?

Before we address the role of WM in comprehension, consider what is meant by the term comprehension. Are you comprehending right now? You are moving your eyes over a page of printed text and, one hopes, deriving some level of understanding or meaning from the process. As a skilled adult reader you can almost certainly "read" without comprehending. You can, for example, read aloud the sentence "'Twas brillig, and the slithy toves did gyre and gimble in the wabe; all mimsy were the borogoves and the mome raths outgrabe" without having any idea what Lewis Carroll meant when he wrote these so-called words.

Comprehension can be thought of as making sense of what we hear or read. But "making sense" has been defined differently by the various researchers who have studied comprehension. As Steven Schwartz (1984) said about comprehension in his book on reading competency, "For some, it means being able to extract the main idea of a passage. For others, making sense of a passage means being able to answer simple questions about it; and for still others, drawing inferences from what is read is the hallmark of comprehension" (p. 99). It is quite likely that you, as the reader, would process a passage differently if you knew you were going to be asked to retain a simple gist of the passage than if you knew you were going to be asked questions requiring the retention of specific facts and details or if you were reading for the simple pleasure of reading with no goal necessarily to recall the material later. What does it say about comprehension if you cannot recall that Schwartz was the author of the last quote but could tell me what the quote means or, conversely, if you could recall that Schwartz was the author but have no idea what he meant by the quote? Thus, comprehension can mean different things at different times, depending on the goal of the reader. As such, the role of WM in comprehension will also vary as a function of the goals of the reader.

We will tell you now some of our ultimate conclusions. It is probably the case that WM would not be important to comprehension if we were only speaking about adults, skilled in comprehending the language being presented to them, and if all spoken and written language were: (1) simple, active, affirmative sentences of relatively few words; (2) there was never a need to retain the specific words spoken previously in order to understand the specific meaning of a currently spoken word; (3) there was never any ambiguity in words or phrases that might lead to misinterpretation, which would hurt comprehension of words spoken or read later; (4) the structure of the "story" we were reading or hearing occurred in a linear fashion with no twists or turns; (5) the structure of the story could be built in a straightforward linear way, with each new element or proposition added to the gist of the story without the need to retain elements that might later have to be discarded; and (6) when seeing or hearing this language, we are not distracted by other events happening in our environment. Of course, much of the language that we process in the modern world is not of the simple and boring type just described. It is for all those other language situations that WM will likely be important.

We will discuss comprehension in the context of the three elements of Baddeley and Hitch's (1974) model of WM: the visuo-spatial sketch-pad, the phonological loop, and the central executive. We have chosen this approach more for convenience than for theoretical motivation. This approach is convenient because most research on working memory, and subsequently, on working memory and comprehension, has been conducted in the context of the Baddeley and Hitch model. Therefore, following this format provides a context for the reader. However, we do not want our approach to suggest that we necessarily agree with the structural distinctions between slave systems, such as the phonological loop and the visuo-spatial sketch-pad. On the contrary, we tend to favour a view in which the structure of the slave systems is consistent, but what varies is the nature of the representation maintained by the system (cf. Cowan, 1995; Engle & Oransky, 1997). Representations can be maintained in many different formats; acoustic, phonological, articulatory, visual, spatial, orthographic, lexical, semantic, etc. We would speculate that there are myriad possible formats that can be maintained by the same structure, and that structure will have the same properties regardless of what type of format is maintained. Thus, "the distinctness and noninterchangeability of phonetic and spatial information occurs because different types of features are being activated, not because of distinctly different storage modules" (Cowan, 1995, p. 36).

THE VISUO-SPATIAL SKETCH-PAD AND COMPREHENSION

We will discuss the role of the visuo-spatial sketch-pad in comprehension first. This type of representation is typically thought of as coding the visual and spatial features of an event—what you might think of as a mental image. In answering the question "Is a pencil longer than a cigarette?" you might form a visual image of the two objects and base your answer to the question on the mental picture. Or suppose you read the following passage: "Nantoo leaned perilously over the edge of the rock and looked out over the huge lake. As his eyes scanned the horizon of diamonds shimmering on the water, he saw the revered eagle. It flew as an arrow to the jewelled surface, then rose with food for its young. An early spring breeze chilled him as he thought of his own efforts to feed his family." It is hard to read a passage such as this without thinking of what the scene "looks" like and "feels" like. In your mind's eye, you can probably see what Nantoo is wearing and what the lake looks like and how far away the eagle is from where Nantoo is standing even though none of that is conveyed in the words. In your mind's heart, you can probably feel what Nantoo feels about feeding his family. Writers of poetry and prose are often judged by how well they can make us "see" and "feel".

The visual and spatial representation is almost certainly a consequence of much of the language we read and hear, but is this type of coding *necessary* for comprehension? Again, the answer probably depends on how we define comprehension. For example, Levin (1973) had 10- to 11-year-old children, who were classified as poor readers, read a 12-sentence story. The children were then asked questions about the details of the passage. Children in one group were trained to form a mental image of the events in each sentence as the passage was read, and other children were simply told to remember what they read because they would be asked questions about it later. The group that was trained to think about the passage using the visuo-spatial code performed better on the test of details. The finding that at least some types of poor readers can be helped if they are trained to use mental imagery is a reliable finding (Pressley, 1976). There is also a relationship between the comprehensibility of prose passages and the ease with which they elicit mental images. Goetz, Sadoski, Fatemi, and Bush (1994) found, for example, that newspaper articles that were rated most comprehensible and understandable were also rated as most likely to lead to a mental image.

But is the visuo-spatial code necessary for comprehension at the level of the individual sentence? An elegant set of studies by Glass, Millen, Beck, and Eddy (1985) addressed this question. They had subjects read, or listen to, high- and low-imagery sentences like "The stars on the American flag are white" and "Biology is the study of living matter". The subjects' task was to verify whether or not the sentence was true. A typical finding on this task is that high-imagery sentences take longer to verify than low-imagery sentences if they are read, but *not* if they are heard. One theory for why this interaction occurs is that comprehension of the high-imagery sentences requires the construction of a visuo-spatial image and that reading, an act requiring visual processing, interferes with this process, thus slowing the construction of the image. Listening, the theory argues, does not interfere with the construction of the visual image. Glass and his colleagues attempted to determine the conditions under which the "high–low imagery by modality" interaction in verification times occurred and when it did not. The interaction was found regardless of whether visual presentation was a word at a time or in normal left-to-right fashion and regardless of the rate of presentation. This suggests that the interference occurred because the necessary visual processing in reading interfered with constructing the visual representation. Two other studies demonstrated that the interaction also occurred with sentences rated high in imagery for location in space such as the following sentence about baseball: "A right-handed hitter places his right side towards the pitcher." This and the earlier findings suggest that the representation used to verify the sentences is a visual and spatial code much like the type of representation maintained by what Baddeley and his colleagues refer to as the visuo-spatial sketch-pad (Baddeley, 1986). But the findings thus far do not say whether the visuo-spatial code is necessary for the comprehension of the sentences *or* for the verification of the truth value of the sentence.

In a crucial experiment to answer this question Glass et al. had subjects judge whether high- and low-visual-imagery sentences were meaningful or not. The sentences were either meaningful, such as "His shirt looked like a giant checkerboard", or not meaningful, such as "A baseball team has nine flavors' and the subject was to rapidly judge the meaningfulness of each sentence. The critical finding was that the high–low imagery by presentation modality interaction was not significant, showing that reading did not hurt comprehension of the high-imagery sentences, at least if comprehension is defined as the ability to say that a string of words makes sense. Thus, Glass et al. concluded that the visuo-spatial code was necessary to judge the truthfulness of a sentence like "Is a pencil longer than a cigarette?" but not to comprehend the sentence.

On the basis of the meagre research on the role of the visuo-spatial representation and comprehension, we would conclude that the type of coding we call the visuo-spatial sketch-pad is useful in many forms of reading and language comprehension, that it is certainly necessary for making comparisons about the objects described by the language, that it even adds to our enjoyment of the language. However, if we define comprehension as whether the language makes sense, then the sketch-pad is probably not necessary for comprehension.

ROLE OF THE PHONOLOGICAL LOOP

In the following section we will use the term "phonological loop" to refer to the slave system of WM responsible for the storage of verbal information. In Baddeley's (1986) model, the phonological loop refers to a system that includes a phonological store coupled with an articulatory loop (Vallar & Baddeley, 1984; 1987). The phonological store maintains short-lived representations resulting from speech-based coding and appears to be particularly important in the retention of order information. The articulatory loop is required to refresh the quickly decaying representations maintained in the phonological store. The loop is also required to transform non-phonological input such as printed words or pictures into a phonological form to be maintained in the store.

That said, we should note the distinction between spoken and written language comprehension. Comprehension of written language has the added dimension of transforming printed words into a form of representation that can be manipulated by a WM system (i.e., phonological store). As such, comprehension of written language makes an added demand on the articulatory-loop component of WM. This is not to say that the articulatory loop is not necessary for comprehension of spoken language. We will argue that the loop is required for maintenance of phonological information during comprehension. Thus, when we refer to "comprehension" we assume both spoken-language and written-language comprehension.

When we read, we often have the intuition that we can hear our inner voice saying the words as we progress through the text. Our intuition suggests that we translate language into some form of memory representation, be it echoic, phonological, or articulatory. Our intuition also tells us that this memory trace is very short-lived. If this book was taken from you right now and you were asked to recall the words of this sentence, you could probably do so without much difficulty. However, if you were asked to recall the words from the first sentence of this paragraph, you would have a problem and would probably make errors. Support for this intuition was provided in a series of experiments by Jarvella (1970, 1971). Subjects listened to passages and were periodically asked to recall the portion of text just presented. The syntactic structure of the passages was manipulated such that the to-be-recalled information was either from the most recent sentence or from an earlier sentence. For example, in the passage, "With this possibility, Taylor left the capital. After he had returned to Manhattan, he explained the offer to his wife." The subject was instructed to recall all the information after the word "After". In this condition all of the to-be-recalled information is included in the last sentence. However, in the passage, "Taylor did not reach a decision until after he had returned to Manhattan. He explained the offer to his wife", the to-be-recalled information "after he had returned from Manhattan" is not included in the most recent sentence. Jarvella (1971) found that retention of the phrase "after he had returned to Manhattan" was poorer if it occurred prior to the sentence boundary. This finding suggests that verbatim information about language is temporarily maintained in an active, readily accessible form, that some form of removal of (or failure to maintain) the information occurs at the sentence boundary, and thus, this information is more difficult to retrieve after the sentence boundary. Jarvella's (1970; 1971) work demonstrated that when readers are asked to do a verbatim recall of what they are reading, they do, in fact, maintain a short-term memory trace of the material they are reading, at least up to the sentence boundary. But it did not demonstrate that the memory trace is phonological or that the phonological loop is necessary to maintain that trace. More importantly, it did not demonstrate that the phonological loop is necessary for comprehension or understanding of what is being read.

If maintaining prior sentence information does, in fact, require use of the phonological loop, then disrupting the function of the loop through articulatory suppression should hurt comprehension. Baddeley, Eldridge, and Lewis (1981) had subjects read sentences and verify whether each sentence was semantically acceptable. For half of the sentences the subjects were instructed to count repeatedly from one to six at a rate of four digits per second while reading. This procedure, called articulatory suppression, has been shown to disrupt the articulatory loop. Baddeley et al. (1981) found that articulatory suppression interfered with comprehension such that subjects were less accurate at judging sentences when they were simultaneously articulating (also see Waters, Caplan, & Hildebrandt, 1987). Thus, it does appear that the phonological loop is necessary for comprehension.

Developmental investigations of children's comprehension also illustrate the importance of the role of the articulatory loop in language comprehension. Donald Shankweiler and his colleagues have argued that children who are classified as good readers perform better than poor readers because they have superior verbal-memory abilities. Importantly, Shankweiler and his colleagues have ruled out alternative hypotheses that differences in reading and listening comprehension are due to differences in knowledge structure, such as different syntactic or phonological knowledge (Mann, Shankweiler, & Smith, 1984; Shankweiler & Crain, 1986; Shankweiler, Smith, & Mann, 1984; Smith, Mann, & Shankweiler, 1986). For example, Mann et al. (1984) classified children as either good or poor readers, based on their performance on the reading subtest of the Iowa Test of Basic Skills, and then compared their listening-comprehension ability on a range of sentence types. The sentences varied in syntactic structure but did not differ in length. The four sentence types were as follows:

1. The sheep pushed the cat that jumped over the cow.
2. The sheep that pushed the cat jumped over the cow.
3. The sheep pushed the cat that the cow jumped over.
4. The sheep that the cat pushed jumped over the cow.

The children were presented with toy actors (i.e. a sheep, a cat, and a cow) and instructed to demonstrate what they heard in each sentence. The dependent variable was comprehension accuracy, which was based on the child's ability to demonstrate correctly the events described in the sentence.

There was a main effect for sentence type, such that sentences of type 1 and 4 caused the most errors. There was also a main effect for reading group, such that the poor readers performed worse than the good readers. More importantly, there was not an interaction between reading group and sentence type. The lack of interaction suggests that the poor readers did not have a deficit specific to one type of syntactic structure. They were simply worse on all types of sentences. Poor readers were also inferior to the good readers in immediate recall of the sentences and on other tests of short-term recall. Thus, it appears that the difference between the good and poor readers was due to differences in short-term or WM. It is not clear whether the differences in performance can be attributed to the phonological loop or to the central executive or to both. However, we should note that the children in the good and poor reading groups were equated for IQ. Given the relationship between central executive processes and IQ (Engle, Tuholski, Laughlin, Conway, 1997), it seems plausible to attribute the differences in these children to differences in phonological processing.

Another way to investigate the specific role of the phonological loop in language comprehension is to study patients who have phonological processing deficits as a result of brain injury.[1] A number of case studies have been reported in the literature and the evidence is remarkably consistent (see Caplan & Waters, 1990, for a review). First, when sentences are short and do not contain complex syntactic structures, such as passive constructions or centre-embedded clauses, patients comprehend as well as normal controls. Patients do have trouble when the syntax becomes more complex, as with passive constructions (e.g. "The boy was pushed by the girl") or centre-embedded clauses ("The man the boy hit carried the box") (Friedrich, Martin, & Kemper, 1985; Saffran & Marin, 1975). Patients also have trouble with sentences that are semantically reversible such as "The cat is chased by the dog" (Caramazza, Basili, Koller, & Berndt, 1981; Caramazza, Berndt, Basili, & Koller, 1981). Another widely reported finding is that patients have difficulty performing the Token Test (Caplan & Waters, 1990), which requires the manipulation of geometrically shaped coloured objects in response to verbal demands. The test varies from simple commands such as "Touch the large white circle" to more difficult commands such as "Put the red circle between the yellow square and the green square." Patients with damage leading to a disturbance of the phonological loop typically perform well when the commands are short and simple but do badly when the commands are long and complex. This

---

[1] For the sake of simplicity and brevity, we will gloss over the distinction between patients with disturbances to the phonological store and those with disturbances to the articulatory loop. For a discussion of this distinction the reader is referred to Caplan and Waters (1990).

suggests that the phonological loop is only required for comprehension when sentences are long or when they contain complex syntactic structures. The problem with the Token Test is that syntactic complexity and sentence length are confounded. Thus, it is impossible to distinguish whether difficulty is due to a deficit in syntactic processing or simply the number of words necessarily retained in WM.

Baddeley, Vallar, and Wilson (1987) recognised this confusion and manipulated sentence length while controlling for syntactic complexity. Two patients with brain damage resulting in phonological-loop disturbances read a number of short sentences that contained a range of syntactic structures. The patients had no trouble comprehending any of the short sentences. However, Baddeley et al. (1981) found that when they increased the length of the sentences by adding syntactically simple components such as adjectives and adverbs, comprehension performance was reduced to chance levels. They concluded that the phonological loop is used as a "mnemonic window" storing and maintaining sentence information as it is processed. Sentence information is entered into and remains in the phonological store until syntactic processing is complete and the discourse representation is updated. Thus, when propositions and sentences are lengthy, the phonological loop is critical for comprehension.

This conclusion assumes that comprehension does not proceed, on-line, as each word occurs. It assumes that, instead, each word is processed at a superficial level and the phonological representation of each word is maintained until the occurrence of syntactic boundary markers in the form of articles or punctuation marks. The markers lead to syntactic parsing of the words, and, at that point, comprehension of the set of parsed words occurs. In other words, syntactic parsing is not immediate. Rather, it is delayed until sufficient information is encountered to achieve the correct syntactic structure and the information is represented in the phonological loop until parsing is complete. Then comprehension of the words in the recently parsed set occurs. By syntactic parsing we mean the process of converting a string of words into a mental representation that contains information about the syntactic class of individual words in the sentence. Parsing is the process by which the reader determines which word is the subject, object, verb, etc., and the syntactic qualities of groups of words such as noun and verb phrases. Obviously, the correct syntactic structure of a phrase or sentence cannot be made immediately when the first word of a sentence is encountered. However, many researchers have argued that parsing occurs very early in the first pass through a sentence. This leads to cognitive structures being built early in the processing of a phrase or sentence. The particular structure is based on the frequency of and bias for the structure. For example, we typically assume a subject–verb–object structure such as "girl-hit-ball".

The question of how syntactic information is extracted from words and sentences is complex, and currently there is not a single model of syntactic parsing that can account for all the phenomena that have been observed. However, Mitchell (1994), in his extensive review of the parsing literature, concluded in favour of early parsing, meaning that this syntactic representation is constructed on the initial pass through a sentence. Thus, the notion proposed by Baddeley et al. (1987) that parsing is delayed and depends on the phonological loop is questionable. There is considerable evidence that word meaning, for instance, occurs as a result of relatively automatic activation of long-term memory when the word is read (cf. Balota, 1983). Studies on the time that we gaze at a word while reading (cf. Just & Carpenter, 1987) suggest that we spend more time looking at more meaningful and lower-frequency words, which suggests that the words are being processed for meaning at the time the word is being read. The studies do suggest that we pause at the end of the sentence, probably to do final wrap-up and integration processes (Just & Carpenter, 1987).

Martin and Feher (1990) employed a strategy similar to that of Baddeley et al. (1987) and found similar results. However, they came to very different conclusions about the role of the phonological loop in language comprehension. They investigated sentence comprehension in aphasic patients and varied both syntactic complexity and sentence length. They also manipulated the presentation mode, with sentences being presented either auditorily or visually. There were two visual conditions, either limited—a word at a time, or unlimited—all words of the sentence presented at one time. In the visual condition, subjects performed better in the unlimited than limited condition, suggesting that the unlimited condition was less memory demanding than the limited condition. Therefore, the difference between performance in the unlimited and limited modes was used as an index of the memory requirements for each sentence type.

Martin and Feher (1990) found that sentence length interacted with presentation mode. In the limited visual condition, there was a decrement in performance for long sentences but not for short sentences. Furthermore, syntactic complexity did *not* interact with presentation mode, meaning that complexity had the same effect with limited and unlimited presentation. They concluded that the phonological loop *is* necessary for the processing of sentences with a large number of content words, but *is not* necessary for processing of sentence syntax, even complex syntax. They argued that the phonological loop is not necessary for initial parsing into syntactic constituents. The loop is necessary AFTER syntactic analysis has taken place but before the sentence has been fully interpreted. This view differs from that of Baddeley et al. (1987) in that it assumes syntactic parsing occurs immediately at input for all sentence types. This conclusion would fit with the idea that the phonological loop is necessary for the wrap-up and integration processes occurring at the end of the sentence.

Waters, Caplan, and Hildebrandt (1987) used healthy adult subjects to address the issue of whether the phonological loop plays a role in initial syntactic parsing or if it plays a role at a post-syntactic level. In one experiment, subjects were asked to make semantic-acceptability judgements about sentences of four different types. The four types were as follows:

1. It was the gangsters that broke into the warehouse.
2. It was the broken clock that the jeweller adjusted.
3. The man hit the landlord that requested the money.
4. The meat that the butcher cut delighted the customer.

These sentences vary along two dimensions: number of propositions and syntactic complexity. The first two types have one proposition and the second two have two. The second and fourth types are more syntactically complex than the others.

Waters et al. (1987) found that subjects were both slower and less accurate to respond to syntactically complex sentences. They also found an effect for number of propositions. However, there was not an interaction between complexity and number of propositions. Waters et al. argued that the absence of an interaction suggests that these variables affect different stages of processing.

In a second experiment, subjects performed a concurrent memory task while reading the same sentences as in the first experiment. The memory task was similar to the reading-span task (Daneman & Carpenter, 1980). The subject was required to make a semantic-correctness judgement about each sentence in a series and then, at the end of the series of sentences, recall the final word of each sentence. There were from two to six sentences in each series. The purpose of this experiment was to determine if those sentence types that were more difficult to process place greater demands on WM. Three dependent measures were recorded: Number of words recalled, judgement accuracy, and judgement latency. For all three dependent variables there were main effects for syntactic complexity and number of propositions, but the interaction was not significant. Waters et al. concluded that the syntactically complex and the two-proposition sentences placed greater demands on WM than the less complex and shorter sentences. Again, the absence of an interaction suggests that these variables affected different stages of processing.

In a third study, subjects performed a semantic judgement task while concurrently performing an articulatory suppression task of repeatedly saying aloud the digits 1–6. Recall that the suppression task has the purpose of eliminating use of the articulatory loop. In addition, there was a no interference condition and a concurrent tapping condition.

The authors found that articulatory suppression interacted with number of propositions, such that suppression had a larger effect on the time to make a judgement for two-proposition sentences than for one-proposition sentences. However, suppression did NOT interact with syntactic complexity. Therefore, they concluded that the phonological loop does NOT play a role at the initial stages of comprehension, that is, syntactic parsing, but does play a role in later stages of analysis. Thus, the loop would be used to represent or to hold already parsed information for later stages of comprehension, such as resolving ambiguities and finalising the interpretation.

In summary, there are two opposing views regarding the role of the phonological loop in language comprehension. Both views agree that the phonological loop is only required when sentences are long and syntactically complex. The first view, proposed by Baddeley et al. (1987), is that the phonological loop maintains sentence information BEFORE syntactic parsing occurs. The second view is that the phonological loop comes into play AFTER parsing occurs and only when initial first-pass processing is not sufficient for comprehension (Caplan & Waters, 1990; Martin & Feher, 1990; Waters et al., 1987).

Either of these theories could be correct, depending on how parsing works. According to Baddeley et al., the phonological loop acts as a "mnemonic window" maintaining information until enough information is provided for a successful parse. The parser does not immediately commit itself to a single syntactic structure. Thus, when a reader encounters complex or ambiguous structures, syntactic analysis is suspended until enough information is provided as to which form is correct. Baddeley et al. would argue that the phonological loop is required to maintain sentence information during this delay. We will refer to this as the "late parsing" view.

The alternative position is that the phonological loop plays a role in comprehension only as a back-up store to be used when processing cannot proceed on-line. According to this view, syntactic parsing occurs automatically, but the parser chooses the structure that is most common or that is most biased by the previous language. However, sometimes the parser is "garden-pathed" or otherwise biased into choosing an incorrect structure. In this case, off-line, second-pass processes are necessary to correct the initial structure. When these second-pass processes are necessary, the phonological loop will be important for comprehension (Caplan & Waters, 1990; Martin & Feher, 1990; Waters et al., 1987). We will refer to this as the "early-parsing" view.

These two accounts make diametrically opposed assumptions with regard to syntactic processing. According to the "late-parsing" view, parsing can be suspended or delayed until an ambiguity is resolved. According to the "early-parsing" view, parsing occurs automatically on-line, even in the face of syntactic ambiguity.

As of this writing, the data required to tease these positions apart are inconclusive, but the evidence seems to support the early-parsing view. According to the late-parsing view, some analyses must be suspended until a syntactic ambiguity is resolved. Therefore, there should be a cost associated with processing the subsequent region of the sentence containing the information that resolves the ambiguity. That is, there should be a slow-down in reading over the portion of the sentence that resolves an earlier-created ambiguity. Indeed, there is a vast amount of evidence to suggest that there is a cost associated with processing disambiguating text when the less common or subordinate interpretation of the ambiguity turns out to be correct (for a review, see Mitchell, 1994). However, there is less evidence with regard to processing disambiguating text when the dominant interpretation of the ambiguity turns out to be correct. This is the evidence needed to answer this question because BOTH early- and late-parsing theories would predict a cost associated with processing the less dominant interpretation of an ambiguity but only late-parsing theories would predict a cost associated with processing the dominant interpretation of an ambiguity.

One study reports no cost associated with processing the dominant interpretation of an ambiguity, relative to an unambiguous control (Mitchell & Cuetos, 1991). This supports the early parsing view. A different study did report an ambiguity effect consistent with the late-parsing view (MacDonald, Just, & Carpenter, 1992). However, the effect was only reported for high-WM-span subjects and other problems have been reported with that study (see Mitchell, 1994; Waters & Caplan, 1996). Furthermore, MacDonald et al. (1992) did not interpret their result as support for a delayed-parsing model. Instead, they suggested that high-span subjects have more central-executive resources than low-span subjects, and are therefore able to build and maintain multiple-syntactic representations while low-span subjects cannot. The maintenance of multiple-syntactic structures will cause high-span readers to read more slowly even after the ambiguity has been presented, and even when the dominant interpretation is correct.

MacDonald et al.'s (1992) claim raises the issue of whether multiple syntactic structures can be built when a syntactic ambiguity is encountered and maintained until the ambiguity is resolved. As an analogy, consider the case of lexical ambiguity.[2] Many authors have argued that multiple

---

[2] We would like to thank Kathy Binder for suggesting this analogy.

meanings of a lexically ambiguous word are activated and maintained until the ambiguity is resolved (Onifer & Swinney, 1981; Swinney, 1979). This claim has been supported by an experimental manipulation called "cross-modal" priming. In a cross-modal priming task, subjects listen to sentences that contain a lexically ambiguous words, such as "There was a bug in the room." Immediately after the lexically ambiguous word (i.e. "bug") has been spoken, the subject is presented with a word on a computer screen and instructed to make a lexical decision. The word presented for lexical decision is either related to one interpretation of the ambiguous word (i.e. "ant"), another interpretation (i.e. "spy"), or neither interpretation (i.e. "sew"). Using these materials, Swinney (1979) found that both "ant" and "spy" were primed by the word "bug", suggesting that both meanings had been activated.

In the case of syntactic ambiguity, evidence of this kind has not been presented. The problem is that there has not been an experimental procedure developed, like cross-modal priming, that demonstrates that multiple syntactic representations are active as MacDonald et al. (1992) argue. Until such evidence is presented, it is not clear whether multiple representation can be formed or not. Therefore, on the basis of the evidence available with regard to syntactic parsing, we are inclined to favour the view that syntactic parsing occurs automatically, on-line, and that the structure that is most common, given the prior sentence information, is initially built.

In the context of our discussion of parsing, we agree with Caplan and Waters (1990), who argued that the phonological loop is not required for automatic, first-pass language comprehension, including syntactic parsing. The phonological loop is required, however, when the first-pass processing is insufficient for comprehension and second-pass processing is necessary for successful comprehension *and* when the number of content words necessary for comprehension of a structure is large. This view is consistent with our notion that WM is important in tasks that require effortful, controlled processing, but not in tasks that can be performed with automatic processing. It is also likely that the phonological-loop processes are harder to use and more attention-demanding with some types of materials. For example, a sentence that contains many rhyming words would make the phonological loop more attention-demanding. To the extent that controlled, limited-capacity attention is required for the coding formats, either phonological or visual/spatial, then the central executive would play a more prominent role in comprehension. The more attention-demanding the situation, the more the central executive would be involved and necessary for comprehension. Thus, those situations placing most burden on the phonological loop would also place most burden on the central executive.

ROLE OF THE CENTRAL EXECUTIVE

Of the three elements of the Baddeley and Hitch (1974) model, the central executive has, until recently, received the least conceptual and empirical development. There is considerable overlap among the ideas referred to as central-executive, controlled-effortful attention (Kahneman, 1973; Posner & Snyder, 1975), supervisory-attentional system (Shallice & Burgess, 1993), working-memory capacity (Daneman & Carpenter, 1980; Conway & Engle, 1994; Engle, Cantor, & Carullo, 1992), and possibly even general fluid intelligence (Kyllonen & Christal, 1990; Engle et al., 1997). It is too early to say whether all of these concepts reflect a common mechanism or are simply related, but recent work from our lab suggests that WM capacity is akin to controlled attention. Thus, before we discuss the role of the central executive in comprehension, we will clarify our view of the central executive (Conway & Engle, 1994; Engle, 1996).

The contents of WM can be conceived of as those memory representations in long-term memory (LTM) that are active beyond some critical threshold. Representations in LTM can become active either because an external event causes activation of the representation or an element of thought automatically spreads activation to the representation. As we wrote earlier, the meaning of a word will likely be activated automatically when the word is read. For the representation of that word to be maintained in an active state, over time, and in the face of subsequent interfering events, the individual must attend to the representation to keep it in the focus of attention (cf. Cowan, 1995). Thus, the amount of information that can be maintained in working memory is limited by the available attentional resources. Please note that this view of working-memory capacity sees the limitation as one of attention, not memory *per se.*

Much of what we consider to be comprehension in the skilled reader is accomplished via automatic spreading activation. For example, the simple occurrence of a printed word in the visual focus will lead to the activation of associations reflecting the meanings of that word. Further, as discussed in the previous section, reading a series of words will likely lead to those words automatically being parsed or given a syntactic structure. We contend that working-memory or central-executive capacity will be important to comprehension whenever the outputs of automatic language processes are insufficient for comprehension and there is confusion either: (1) because of the large number of words in the sentence; (2) because there is ambiguity about the meaning of individual words or phrases; (3) because language early in a passage is misleading about the ultimate meaning of the passage; or (4) because the syntactic structure of the language is unduly complex.

When the language becomes unduly complex, the reader must have the ability to maintain information that is relevant to the passage and block out or suppress information that is irrelevant. Thus, we will focus on two aspects of language comprehension: maintenance of information over a period of time and the suppression of distracting or irrelevant information.

Daneman and Carpenter (1980; 1983) were the first to demonstrate the importance of individual differences in central-executive capacity to comprehension. They reasoned that individuals with large WM capacity should be able to maintain more information in an active state at any given time. This would be important to comprehension when sentences are particularly long or when the meaning of a word depends on the retention of information read much earlier. For example, consider the following passage:

> Fred and Bill went to the store to buy groceries. Fred bought a half gallon of ice cream and Bill bought some bread and a bottle of juice. On the way home they were involved in an accident but no one was hurt. After lengthy questioning by the authorities and exchanging insurance information with the driver of the other car, the two went home. When they arrived home, he quickly put the ice cream in the freezer.

When the reader encounters the word "he" in the last sentence, successful comprehension depends on whether the reader can quickly retrieve the information about *who* bought the ice cream. Daneman and Carpenter (1980) reasoned that individuals with larger WM capacity should be more likely to have that information still available when the word "he" is read. They developed a task called the reading-span task, mentioned earlier. In this task, the subject read a set of sentences aloud and then attempted to recall the last word of each sentence in the correct order. The sentence sets varied from two to seven and the maximum number of final words the person could recall correctly was called the reading span score. Those individuals who received a high reading span score were referred to as high working memory and those with a low score were referred to as low working memory.

Daneman and Carpenter (1980) found that high WM subjects correctly answered questions like "Who put the ice cream in the freezer?" better than did low WM subjects. The comprehension difference between low and high WM capacity subjects was even greater if more words separated the pronoun (he) from its noun referent (Fred). Reading span correlated with a variety of reading-comprehension measures including answering fact questions ($r = 0.27$), pronoun reference questions ($r = 0.90$), and even the VSAT ($r = 0.40 - 0.59$).

Clearly, individual differences on the reading-span task covary with important aspects of tests of comprehension. But what is the nature of that covariation? What does the reading span task measure that is important to comprehension? Daneman and Carpenter (1980; 1983) argued that the reading-span score was really an indirect measure of the reading skills of the individual. If reading processes are very efficient and automatic, then more attentional resources are available to retain the final words. To the extent that reading processes are less efficient, there would be less capacity to allocate to retention of the words. By this view, which we have labelled the *task-specific view* of working-memory capacity, the reading span–comprehension correlation is quite specific to tasks involving reading.

An extensive series of studies from our lab has disputed this claim, and we have argued that complex tasks such as reading span reflect general, domain-free attentional resources that will be important in any cognitive task requiring controlled processing, an idea we call the *general-capacity view*. Turner and Engle (1989) used a measure of working-memory capacity called the operation span in which subjects performed sets of arithmetic strings with a word to be recalled later following each string. For example, the subject might see "IS (4/2) − 1 = 1? SNOW", followed by "IS (3 × 1) + 4 = 7? TABLE". The subject would answer "yes" or "no" to indicate whether the given answer is correct or incorrect, read the word aloud, and then do the next string, and so on. After a set of strings (which varied from two to seven strings), the subject would try to recall the words, in this case, SNOW and TABLE. If the task-specific view is correct, then the operation span should not correlate with reading comprehension, because the processes used in the span task are different than those used during reading. However, Turner and Engle (1989) showed that the relationship between reading comprehension and operation span was just as high as between comprehension and reading span. Engle, Cantor, and Carullo (1992) showed that factoring-out skill on the processing component of both the operation span and reading span did not reduce the correlation between the span score and comprehension. Conway and Engle (1996) showed that manipulating the difficulty of the processing component, so that subjects were equated on the difficulty of the processing, did not reduce the correlation between the span score and comprehension. Thus, there is considerable evidence for the idea that complex measures of working-memory capacity reflect general, domain-free attentional resources.

Thus, the resources of the central executive are important for maintaining information over time and in the face of distracting, misleading, or interfering information. A good example of this is when there is ambiguity in the meaning of words or phrases. For example, in the passage below:

The lights in the concert hall were dimmed. The audience watched intently as the famous violinist appeared on the stage. He stepped onto the podium and turned majestically to face the audience. He took a bow. It was very gracefully propped on the music stand. The enthusiastic applause resounded throughout the hall.

Such passages are called "garden path" passages, because the word "bow" has two different pronunciations and two different meanings. If the reader is led to select the incorrect meaning and fails to maintain the correct meaning, comprehension will break down when the reader encounters the sentence that implies that the protagonist grasped a violin bow that was propped on the music stand. Daneman and Carpenter (1983) argued that high WM subjects would be more likely to maintain the original meanings and pronunciation information available when they need to resolve the ambiguity, and they would be better than low WM subjects at answering a question such as "What did the violinist take?" They found that, indeed, high-span subjects were better than low spans at disambiguating the sentence. Further, this difference between WM groups was even greater if a sentence boundary occurred between the ambiguous word and the phrase that resolved the ambiguity. Daneman and Carpenter argued that the low WM subjects were more likely to lose the additional meaning of the ambiguous word in the wrap-up and integration processing that occurs at the end of each sentence.

A more detailed analysis of individual differences in the resolution of lexical ambiguity supports these results. Miyake, Just, and Carpenter (1994) had high- and low-WM span subjects read sentences that contained lexical ambiguities. Previous research suggested that when a lexical ambiguity is encountered, multiple meanings are automatically activated (Onifer & Swinnery, 1981; Swinney, 1979), and remain active until the ambiguity is resolved, at which point the correct interpretation of the ambiguous word is integrated into the discourse structure and the inappropriate meaning either decays or is actively suppressed (Simpson, 1984). Miyake et al. (1994) proposed that individual differences in WM capacity will not play a role in accessing the meanings of the ambiguous word because activating multiple meanings occurs automatically (Onifer & Swinney, 1981; Swinney, 1979). However, individual differences in WM capacity will play a role if multiple meanings need to be maintained over a period of time. Therefore, if the ambiguity remains unresolved for a period of time, low-span subjects will not abe able to maintain multiple meanings, which will cause confusion when the ambiguity is finally resolved.

Miyake et al. (1994) presented subjects with sentences such as the following, "Since Ken really liked the boxer, he took a bus to the nearest pet store to buy the animal.' Note that the word "boxer" is ambiguous and the ambiguity is not resolved until the phrase "pet store". The word "boxer" is considered a "biased" ambiguous word because one interpretation (fighter) is more common than the other interpretation (dog). We will refer to the common interpretation as the dominant interpretation and the less common interpretation as the subordinate interpretation. According to Miyake et al., high- and low-span subjects activate both the dominant and the subordinate meanings when they encounter an ambiguous word. High-span subjects are then able to maintain both meanings until the ambiguity is resolved. By contrast, low-span subjects are only able to maintain the dominant meaning. Thus, when the subordinate meaning of the ambiguous word turns out to be the correct interpretation, as in the sentence, "Since Ken really liked the boxer, he took a bus to the nearest pet store to buy the animal", high-span subjects will not be adversely affected when the ambiguity is resolved because they will have the subordinate meaning active. By contrast, low-span subjects will be affected when the ambiguity is resolved because they will no longer have the subordinate meaning active.

Consistent with their predictions, Miyake et al. (1994) found that when the subordinate meaning turned out to be the correct interpretation, low-span subjects showed increased reading times in the disambiguating region of the sentence, while high-span subjects did not. Their conclusion was that both high- and low-span subjects activate multiple meanings of an ambiguous word, but that only high-span subjects are able to maintain both representations. Low-span subjects only maintain the dominant meaning.

An implicit assumption of this analysis is that both low and high working-memory subjects activated both meanings of the ambiguous word. Miyake et al. (1994) did not test this assumption. It is therefore possible that low-span subjects never activated the subordinate meaning of the ambiguous words. Low-WM subjects almost certainly have less word knowledge than high-WM subjects (Dixon, LeFevre, & Twilley, 1988; Engle, Nations, & Cantor, 1990), and so might have less access to the low-dominance meanings of homographs. Thus, the low WM subjects may not have activated the lower-frequency meanings. In fact, Deaton, Gernsbacher, Robertson, and Miyake (1995) presented evidence to suggest that low-span subjects do not activate the subordinate meaning of lexically ambiguous words. If so, then the results of the Miyake, et al. (1994) study occurred because of an effect at the stage of lexical access, not in the maintenance of information, and the effect was not really a result of differences in working memory.

Therefore, just as we ended our discussion of syntactic ambiguity, we will end here with a word of caution. Although it is possible that Miyake et al.'s (1994) interpretation is correct, more research is needed to establish whether low-span subjects do in fact activate multiple meanings of ambiguous words. Insofar as activation of meaning is automatic, we would argue that they do activate multiple meanings. However, if the subordinate meaning of an ambiguous word is not well known, then the process of activating that meaning may not be automatic, which means that WM capacity may then play a role in lexical access. As an analogy, consider a child learning to read. When the child encounters a relatively novel word, accessing the meaning of that word may involve a conscious, effortful process that would demand attention. However, as the child becomes more familiar with that word, accessing the meaning will no longer require a controlled effortful process. Given the fact that low-WM span subjects have weaker vocabulary knowledge than high-span readers (Engle et al., 1990), it is possible that for low-span readers the activation of the subordinate meaning of an ambiguous word is not entirely automatic, and therefore may not occur when attention is directed elsewhere.

Not only is the central executive necessary for maintaining relevant information, it is also important for suppressing irrelevant information that is not needed for comprehension and would otherwise add confusion to the meaning of the passage. Gernsbacher and colleagues (Gernsbacher, 1990; Gernsbacher & Faust, 1991; Gernsbacher, Varner, & Faust, 1990) have studied the role of suppression in comprehension. They hypothesised that individuals who are poor comprehenders (who, given the correlation between WM capacity and reading comprehension, are likely to also be low-WM individuals) are less adept at suppressing contextually irrelevant information than are good comprehenders. Gernsbacher et al. (1990) had subjects read sentences such as "He dug with the spade." Notice that spade can be either an implement for digging or a card suit. Either immediately after, or one second after the sentence, the subjects were presented with a probe word, such as "car", "shovel", or "ace". The subject's task was quickly to respond "yes" or "no" to indicate whether the probe word was consistent with the meaning of the sentence. If both meanings of spade are activated when the sentence is read, then it should be more difficult for the subject to determine that the probe word "ace" is not consistent with the sentence than it would be for the subject to determine that "car" is not consistent with the sentence. Indeed, Gernsbacher et al. (1990) found that if the probe word was presented immediately after the sentence, both good and poor comprehenders were slower to say that "ace" was not related to the meaning of the sentence than they were to say that "car" was not related to the meaning of the sentence. If the probe was presented one second after the sentence, good comprehenders were no longer slowed, suggesting that they were able to suppress the irrelevant meaning of the ambiguous word. By contrast, poor comprehenders were slowed just as much after the one-second delay as they were when the probe was presented immediately after the sentence. This suggests that poor comprehenders did not suppress the irrelevant meaning of the ambiguous word. Presumably, keeping irrelevant meanings active will ultimately interfere with comprehension because multiple-semantic structures will be possible and the simple presence of irrelevant information in WM will lead to interference and depletion of resources.

The work of Miyake et al. (1994) and Gernsbacher (1990) at first appear to suggest two contradictory characteristics of individuals with poor central-executive capacities. Miyake et al.'s results suggest that low-span subjects cannot maintain multiple meanings over a brief period of time, whereas Gernsbacher's results suggest that low-span subjects cannot suppress irrelevant meanings, which results in irrelevant meanings remaining active and causing confusion. We submit here that both of these proposals are, in fact, compatible with our notion (Conway & Engle, 1994; Engle, 1996) that both maintenance and suppression of information require attentional resources, and sentences can be constructed such that either suppression or maintenance will best serve comprehension. For example, in the sentence, "Since Ken really liked the boxer he took a bus to the nearest pet store to buy the animal", comprehension will be served better if both meanings of the ambiguous word are maintained until the ambiguity is resolved. However, once the ambiguity is resolved, the irrelevant meaning should be suppressed, so that it does not interfere with the correct interpretation of the sentence. Thus, in Gernsbacher's experiment, after reading, "He dug with the spade", the irrelevant meaning of "spade" (ace) should be suppressed immediately to avoid confusion and to clear working memory of irrelevant and potentially distracting information.

If the central executive is defined in terms of the ability to bring controlled attention to bear on the task at hand and individuals differ in that ability, then high-WM subjects can and will either maintain or suppress information, depending on which is deemed more appropriate for the task being performed at the moment. We submit that experiments could be designed in such a way as to encourage maintenance or suppression, and high-WM subjects would respond accordingly. Low-WM subjects, particularly if the comprehension task were already attention-demanding, would be less able to do the appropriate maintenance or suppression.

This hypothesis could be tested with regard to either syntactic ambiguity or lexical ambiguity. A number of variables could be manipulated in conjunction with ambiguity and WM span. For example, the time course of the ambiguity could be manipulated, such that the ambiguity is either immediately resolved or resolved after a number of words or phrases. Also, the local and global context surrounding the ambiguity could be manipulated to see if high- and low-WM-span subjects use contextual information differently. Experimenters could manipulate the type of ambiguity, with either equally biased ambiguities, where each meaning or structure is equally likely given the preceding context, or biased ambiguities where one meaning or structure is the dominant interpretation and the other is subordinate. With this manipulation, one could test the possibility that high- and low-span subjects differ in their ability to activate multiple meanings or form multiple representations. This last point is especially important. That is, in order to test whether high- and low-span subjects differ in the maintenance or suppression of information, it must first be demonstrated that both high- and low-span subjects have the critical information active. Until that has been established, one cannot test for individual differences in maintenance or suppression.

Finally, we would submit that even high-WM-span subjects may sometimes perform like low-WM-span subjects, if they are burdened with a demanding workload. What would constitute a mental workload in real-life comprehension situations? Our intuition suggests that trying to read in a situation where there is much distraction, such as in a college dormitory or while trying to watch a television programme, would constitute a workload. A young man trying to listen to and comprehend what is said when he first meets his new girlfriend's father is under the added workload of the emotional pressure of worrying about making a good impression. We would argue that even high-WM subjects should not be able to suppress irrelevant meanings or maintain information for very long if they are trying to comprehend language under such circumstances.

CONCLUSION

Is working memory necessary for comprehension? If adults, skilled in reading and listening to speech, are asked to comprehend short, simple, active, affirmative, declarative sentences, and each sentence follows logically and inexorably from the previous one and no ambiguous words or phrases are used, then the collection of structures and processes we have referred to as working memory will not be necessary for comprehension. If there is never any need to retain a verbatim copy of the words we read or hear because those words are never referred to by pronouns, then working memory will not be necessary for comprehension. If we are never interrupted or distracted in the midst of reading or listening then it will not be necessary to maintain representations in an active state and working memory will not be necessary. If there is never a need to suppress or dump irrelevant information to avoid confusion, then working memory will not be necessary. However, it is for all those other situations that we can be grateful that we have the system of representational formats and controlled attention that we call working memory to aid our comprehension of complex language events.

REFERENCES

Baddeley, A.D. (1986). *Working Memory*. Oxford: Clarendon Press.

Baddeley, A.D., & Hitch, G. (1974). Working memory. In G.A. Bower (Ed.), *The psychology of learning and motivation* (Vol. 8, pp. 47–89). New York: Academic Press.

Baddeley, A., Eldridge, M., & Lewis, V. (1981). The role of subvocalisation in reading. *Quarterly Journal of Experimental Psychology, 33A,* 439–454.

Baddeley, A, Vallar, G., & Wilson, B. (1987). Sentence comprehension and phonological memory: Some neuropsychological evidence. In M. Coltheart (Ed.), *Attention and performance: Vol. 12. The psychology of reading* (pp. 509–529). Hove: Lawrence Erlbaum Associates Ltd.

Balota, D.A. (1983). Automatic semantic activation and episodic memory encoding. *Journal of Verbal Learning and Verbal Behavior, 22,* 88–104.

Caplan, D., & Waters, G.S. (1990). Short-term memory and language comprehension: A critical review of the neuropsychological literature. In G. Vallar & T. Shallice (Eds.), *Neuropsychological impairments of short-term memory* (pp. 337–389). Cambridge: Cambridge University Press.

Caramazza, A., Basili, A.G., Koller, J.J., & Berndt, R.S. (1981). An investigation of repetition and language processing in a cases of conduction aphasia. *Brain and Language, 14,* 235–271.

Caramazza, A., Berndt, R.S., Basili, A.G., & Koller, J.J. (1981). Syntactic processing deficits in aphasia. *Cortex, 17,* 333–348.

Conway, A.R.A., & Engle, R.W. (1994). Working memory and retrieval: A resource-dependent inhibition model. *Journal of Experimental Psychology: General, 123,* 354–373.

Conway, A.R.A., & Engle, R.W. (1996). Individual differences in working memory capacity: More evidence for a general capacity theory. *Memory, 4,* 577–590.

Cowan, N. (1995). *Attention and memory: An integrated framework*. Oxford: Oxford University Press.

Daneman, M., & Carpenter, P.A. (1980). Individual differences in working memory and reading. *Journal of Verbal Learning and Verbal Behavior, 19,* 450–466.

Daneman, M., & Carpenter, P.A. (1983). Individual differences in integrating information between and within sentences. *Journal of Experimental Psychology: Learning, Memory, & Cognition, 9,* 561–584.

Deaton, J.A., Gernsbacher, M.A., Robertson, R.R.W., & Miyake, A. (1995). *Working memory span and lexical ambiguity: Problems with lexical access*. Paper presented at the annual meeting of Midwestern Psychological Association, Chicago.

Dixon, P., LeFevre, J., & Twilley, L.C. (1988). Word knowledge and working memory as predictors of reading skill. *Journal of Educational Psychology, 80,* 465–472.

Engle, R.W. (1996). Working memory and retrieval: An inhibition-resource approach. In J.T.E. Richardson, R.W. Engle, L. Hasher, R.H. Logie, E.R. Stoltzfus, & R.T. Zacks (Eds.), *Working memory and human cognition* (pp. 89–119). New York: Oxford University Press.

Engle, R.W., Cantor, J., & Carullo, J.J. (1992). Individual differences in working memory and comprehension: A test of four hypotheses. *Journal of Experimental Psychology: Learning, Memory, and Cognition, 18,* 972–992.

Engle, R.W., & Oransky, N. (in press). The evolution from short-term to working memory: Multi-store to dynamic models of temporary storage. In R.J. Sternberg (Ed.), *The concept of cognition*, Cambridge, MA: MIT Press.

Engle, R.W., Nations, J.K., & Cantor, J. (1990). Is "working memory capacity" just another name for word knowledge? *Journal of Educational Psychology, 82,* 799–804.

Engle, R.W., Tuholski, S.W., Laughlin, J.E., & Conway, A.R.A. (submitted). Working memory, short-term memory and general fluid intelligence: A latent variable approach. *Journal of Experimental Psychology: General.*

Friedrich, F.J., Martin, R., & Kemper, S.J. (1985). Consequences of a phonological coding deficit on sentence processing. *Cognitive Neuropsychology, i2,* 385–412.

Gernsbacher, M.A. (1990). *Language comprehension as structure building.* Hillsdale, NJ: Lawrence Erlbaum Associates Inc.

Gernsbacher, M.A., & Faust, M.E. (1991). The mechanism of suppression: A component of general comprehension skill. *Journal of Experimental Psychology: Learning, Memory, and Cognition, 17,* 245–262.

Gernsbacher, M.A., Varner, K.R., & Faust, M.E. (1990). Investigating differences in general comprehension skill. *Journal of Experimental Psychology: Learning, Memory, and Cognition, 16,* 430–445.

Glass, A.L., Millen, D.R., Beck, L.G., & Eddy, J.K. (1985). Representation of images in sentence verification. *Journal of Memory and Language, 24,* 442–465.

Goetz, E.T., Sadoski, M., Fatemi, Z., & Bush, R. (1994). That's news to me: Reader's responses to brief newspaper articles. *Journal of Reading Behavior, 26,* 125–128.

Jarvella, R.J. (1970). Effects of syntax on running memory span for connected discourse. *Psychonomic Science, 19,* 235–236.

Jarvella, R.J. (1971). Syntactic processing of connected speech. *Journal of Verbal Learning and Verbal Behavior, 10,* 409–416.

Just, M.A., & Carpenter, P.A. (1987). *The psychology of reading and language comprehension.* Boston: Allyn and Bacon.

Kahneman, D. (1973). *Attention and effort.* Englewood Cliffs, NJ: Prentice-Hall.

Kyllonen, P.C., & Christal, R.E. (1990). Reasoning ability is (little more than) working-memory capacity. *Intelligence, 14,* 389–443.

Levin, J.R. (1973). Inducing comprehension in poor readers: A test of a recent model. *Journal of Educational Psychology, 65,* 19–24.

Schwartz, S. (1984). *Measuring reading competence: A theoretical-prescriptive approach.* New York: Plenum Press.

Shallice, T., & Burgess, P. (1993). Supervisory control of action and thought selection. In A.D. Baddeley & L. Weiskrantz (Eds.), *Attention, selection, awareness, and control: A tribute to Donald Broadbent* (pp. 171–187). Oxford: Oxford University Press.

Shankweiler, D., & Crain, S. (1986). Language mechanisms and reading disorder: A modular approach. *Cognition, 24,* 139–168.

Shankweiler, D., Smith, S.T., & Mann, V.A. (1984). Repetition and comprehension of spoken sentences by reading-disabled children. *Brain and Language, 23,* 241–257.

Simpson, G.B. (1984). Lexical ambiguity and its role in models of word recognition. *Psychological Bulletin, 96,* 316–340.

Smith, S.T., Mann, V.A., & Shankweiler, D. (1986). Spoken sentence comprehension by good and poor readers: A study with the token test. *Cortex, 22,* 627–632.

Swinney, D.A. (1979). Lexical access during sentence comprehension: (Re)consideration of context effects. *Journal of Verbal Learning and Verbal Behavior, 18,* 645–659.

Tuholski, S.W., Laughlin, J., Conway, A.R.A., & Engle, R.W. (1997). Do working-memory and short-term memory tasks reflect the same construct? Manuscript submitted for publication.

Turner, M.L., & Engle, R.W. (1989). Is working-memory capacity task dependent? *Journal of Memory and Language, 28,* 127–154.

Vallar, G., & Baddeley, A.D. (1984). Phonological short-term store, phonological processing, and sentence comprehension: A neurological case study. *Cognitive Neuropsychology, 1,* 121–141.

Vallar, G., & Baddeley, A.D. (1987). Phonological short-term store and sentence processing. *Cognitive Neuropsychology, 4*, 417–438.

Waters, G.S., & Caplan, D. (1996). The capacity theory of sentence comprehension: Critique of Just and Carpenter (1992). *Psychological Review, 103*, 761–772.

Waters, G.S., Caplan, D., & Hildebrandt, N. (1987). Working memory and written sentence comprehension. In M. Coltheart (Ed.), *Attention and performance: Vol. 12. The psychology of reading* (pp. 531–555). Hove: Lawrence Erlbaum Associates Ltd.

CHAPTER SIX

Working Memory and Expert Performance

K. Anders Ericsson and Peter F. Delaney
Florida State University, USA

Decades of research on performance in laboratory tasks have revealed general information-processing constraints on the acquisition of skilled performance. The most important constraint concerns the capacity of working memory—the amount of information about the task and generated results that subjects can keep continuously accessible during task-directed performance. Studies of short-term memory (STM) have shown that the amount of information subjects can maintain in temporary storage through rehearsal is very limited and sets limits for the capacity of working memory in laboratory tasks. The basic storage capacity of working memory is assumed to remain fixed and to be invariant across all types of cognitive activity. Models of cognitive processes in many laboratory tasks have shown that with appropriate strategies subjects can successfully execute their cognitive processes within the limited storage capacity of working memory. Even skilled and expert performance is assumed to be constrained by the same capacity limits. Under traditional theories of expert performance (e.g. Chase & Simon, 1973) and skill acquisition (e.g. Anderson, 1982; Fitts & Posner, 1967), superior performance levels attained after practice reflect the reduction of load on working memory through the automatisation of serial processes and the processing of more complex chunks of knowledge. Recently, however, evidence from expert and skilled performance has shown that the amount of information available in working memory can be dramatically increased for specific tasks and that the storage of this information is neither temporary nor critically dependent on active rehearsal.

First, experts and skilled performers are able to maintain a considerable amount of information in an accessible form during processing in domain-relevant tasks. For example, some chess masters are able to play blindfold chess, i.e. without a perceptually available chess board, at master or near-master level (Holding, 1985). A few chess masters have, with additional training in blindfold chess, learned to play against more than 20 highly skilled opponents and still win most of the games (Koltanowski, 1985). Some lightning mental calculators are able to multiply pairs of large numbers, such as 562,803,144*9,878, without any external memory aids (Jensen, 1990; Smith, 1983).

Second, expert and skilled performance often can be resumed after a disruption without significant effects on the resumed performance. Similarly, concurrent activities ("dual tasks") typically have at most minor effects on working memory during expert performance. For example, an expert waiter was able to engage in unrelated conversation while memorising dinner orders for up to 16 people (Ericsson & Polson, 1988a; 1988b). Skilled chess-players' memories for chessboard configurations are essentially unaffected by disruptions of unrelated attention-demanding tasks (Charness, 1976; Saariluoma, 1991a; 1991b). Hence, expert performance is far more interruptible than would be predicted from the assumption that they have to maintain all of the temporarily stored information in working memory by continued rehearsal.

Finally, experts and skilled performers are able accurately to recall information about presented tasks when tested unexpectedly at the end of a session. For example, the amount of recall for previously seen problems increases as a function of chess skill in chess players (Charness, 1981a; Lane & Robertson, 1979) and as a function of expertise in medical experts (Norman, Brooks, & Allen, 1989). Taken together, these facts point to some more stable form of working memory than that postulated by the traditional view of working memory.

Recent reviews of expert performance (Ericsson & Charness, 1994; Ericsson, Krampe, & Tesch-Römer, 1993) have shown that experts engage in thousands of hours of deliberate practice in order to acquire support skills that let them circumvent many types of capacity limits. A recent paper by Ericsson and Kintsch (1995) has explicitly shown how experts and highly skilled individuals can circumvent the limited capacity of working memory through the use of skills that allow rapid, reliable storage of information in long-term memory (LTM). Under their proposal, experts store potentially useful domain-related information in LTM and index it with specific retrieval cues. By keeping these retrieval cues in the short-term portion of working memory (ST-WM), experts can maintain indirect access to much more information stored in LTM. This *long-term working memory* (LT-WM) is a set of acquired mechanisms that enables experts to expand the functional capacity of their working-memory system for specific types of materials in activities within their domain of expertise without altering the general capacity limits of ST-WM.

In this chapter, we will describe working memory in expert performance based on LT-WM (Ericsson & Kintsch, 1995). We will begin with a historical review of research on memory that led investigators to believe that working memory could only reflect storage in ST-WM, because storage in LTM was found to be too slow and unreliable. Then we will review research on the effects of training of memory performance to show how rapid and reliable storage in LTM can be attained through the acquisition of specific mediating mechanisms. Next, we consider how this idea can be extended to account for working memory in experts and highly skilled performers. Finally, we consider how the informational demands of a task lead to the development of particular memory skills, and close with some implications for future research.

THE SEARCH FOR BASIC MEMORY CAPACITY IN THE LABORATORY

As early as Ebbinghaus' (1885/1964) laboratory-based studies of memory it was already known that the effectiveness of memory for newly encountered information was improved when it could be related to prior knowledge and experience. Any theoretical account of memory performance would thus have to identify all of an individual's relevant knowledge—a virtually impossible task for both practical and theoretical reasons. Ebbinghaus' (1885/1964) solution was to control for the effects of prior experience, or at least minimise them, through the use of unfamiliar materials (nonsense syllables) and a rapid presentation rate for individual items. Using this methodology, he and his successors were able to generate many reproducible relations and "laws" of memorisation and forgetting.

With the emergence of cognitive psychology in the 1950s and 1960s, Ebbinghaus' basic technique of controlling for prior knowledge through the use of what Chaiken (1994) has termed "content-free processing tasks" yielded new information about the capacity and size of the components of memory. These components composed the invariant "hardware", as distinct from the malleable "software" of knowledge and skill. Short-term memory, in this context, was primarily assessed using a memory-span task where subjects were briefly presented with short lists of randomly selected words and numbers, and asked to reproduce all the items in perfect order. Miller (1956) observed that this method produced convergent estimates of STM capacity across a broad range of stimulus materials, generally around seven chunks. Each chunk in STM corresponded to a familiar pattern in LTM, typically an individual item such as a word or digit. In certain cases, familiar combinations of items had been previously grouped together and once stored as patterns in LTM they could function and be treated as a single unit or "chunk" in STM. The extensive laboratory-research findings on memory performance were eventually integrated into a theory of memory, which featured distinct memory stores with different storage and retrieval characteristics (Atkinson & Shiffrin, 1968).

When Newell and Simon (1972) proposed the information-processing theory of human cognition, they relied on the results of the memory research to identify general capacity constraints on information-processing models. The most crucial of these constraints was the amount of information that could be maintained with near-perfect reliability during problem-solving (working memory). Because thinking generally relies on many intermediate products that are only briefly needed to produce new intermediate products, the rate of information flow through memory tends to be quite high. This rapid flow was believed to be too fast to allow for effective use of LTM for such information, and hence the upper bound on working-memory size would be the size of STM. In practice, the actual capacity of working memory was found to be even smaller, around four chunks (Broadbent, 1975). Even with this severe capacity limit, investigators were able to design simulation models that accounted for performance on a range of novel laboratory tasks, including novice problem-solving (Atwood & Polson, 1976; Newell & Simon, 1972), concept formation (Levine, 1966), and decision-making (Payne, 1976). More recent theorists (Anderson, 1983; Newell, 1990), however, have proposed that the capacity of working memory must be significantly greater to allow computer models to account successfully for skilled performance. Some of Anderson's (1983) simulation models required that as many as 20 units were simultaneously activated in working memory.

In the introduction, we described evidence from expert and skilled performance that even larger amounts of information can be maintained in working memory, and that access to much of this information remains after the completion of the task, suggesting storage in LTM. How can we reconcile the expanded capacity of working memory in particular skilled activities with the general limits and characteristics of STM and LTM? Ericsson and Kintsch (1995) have argued that some of the characteristics of these memory stores (especially LTM) uncovered in the laboratory studies using unfamiliar materials and tasks will not remain invariant, as subjects have the opportunity to acquire high levels of performance in a particular task domain. Their proposal for long-term working memory (LT-WM) postulated that subjects were able to acquire domain-specific skills to store rapidly task-relevant information in LTM and maintain access to this stored information via retrieval cues in STM. This proposal would appear to violate some of the characteristics attributed to LTM based on memory for unfamiliar materials, which are listed in Table 6.1.

In the remainder of this chapter, we will report evidence from expert performance for rapid and reliable storage in LTM of domain-specific information, in contrast with the slow and unreliable storage in LTM for any type of unfamiliar information. The most important distinction between cognitive processing in an unfamiliar and highly familiar task is that skilled subjects know the structure and the memory demands of the task. Hence, skilled individuals can selectively identify the information that will be needed for future processing as well as anticipate under which circumstances the information will be used. At the time of original encoding of information in LTM they can therefore associate particular retrieval cues that allow them to later access that information by activating the corresponding retrieval cues. Additional retrieval cues and associations may be created through integrative processing and inference generation, providing protection against interference and forgetting.

In the following section, we will report on Chase and Ericsson's (1981; 1982) research on the acquisition of exceptional memory performance on the prototypical task for measurement of the capacity of STM. We will describe the acquired mechanisms that allow trained subjects to use LTM for reliable storage and retrieval of information without violating general capacity limits for human information-processing. Then we will review evidence from expert performance showing similar mechanisms supporting LT-WM in several domains of expertise.

IMPROVED MEMORY PERFORMANCE THROUGH TRAINING ON TASKS ASSUMED TO MEASURE CAPACITY OF STM

The best evidence for the claim that the functional capacity of working memory can be increased for particular kinds of information comes from

TABLE 6.1

Long-term memory characteristics based on memory performance with unfamiliar materials and characteristics for storage in LT-WM for domain-related information

Property	LTM in unfamiliar tasks	LT-WM
Generality	General across materials	Only practised materials
Required time for storage	5–10 seconds[a]	Rapid storage
Reliability of storage	Probabilistic	Accurate
Criteria for storage in LTM	Minimal	Highly selective
Anticipation of retrieval demands	Minimal	High

[a] Simon (1976).

training studies using the memory-span task. Chase and Ericsson (1981; 1982) reported that two subjects with digit spans in the normal range (around seven digits) were able gradually to increase their digit spans to a level surpassing that of most professional memorists (around 15–20 digits). One of these subjects eventually attained a digit span of 82 digits after about 200 hours of practice distributed over two years (Chase & Ericsson, 1981; 1982), whereas the other was eventually able to recall lists of 104 digits after over 800 daily practice sessions distributed over 3 years (Richman, Staszewski, & Simon, 1995; Staszewski, 1988). Additional subjects with less than 100 hours of practice were able to achieve digit spans of 20 or more (Ericsson, 1988).

These large improvements in memory performance are consistent with a requirement for training (see Table 6.1). Furthermore, the increase in memory span was specific to digits, and did not generalise to other types of materials. Memory span for consonants, for instance, remained in the normal range (Ericsson, Chase, & Faloon, 1980; Staszewsi, 1988).

Ordinary digit-span performance is assumed to involve only STM, with very little if any involvement of LTM. Consistent with this, the digit-span experts showed rehearsal strategies typical of STM storage prior to training. As they accumulated practice, however, they began to make increasing use of LTM for storage and retrieval. After a test session that involved the presentation of several digit lists, the experts were asked to recall as much as possible from the entire session. They were generally able accurately to recall 90% of the presented digits. Furthermore, when one of the subjects was forced to engage in a demanding task for 30 seconds following the presentation, but prior to recall, the disruption had only minimal effects on recall (Chase & Ericsson, 1981).

The digit-span task directly addresses issues about speed of storage and accuracy of recall when using LTM, because the speed of presentation remains fixed at 1 digit/s and the criterion for success (correct recall) requires perfect reproduction of the digits in order. In addition, Chase and Ericsson (1982) found that, after substantial training, subjects were able to memorise lists of digits shorter than their maximum span at presentation rates much faster than 1 digit/s. These experiments yielded estimates of the necessary time to store items in LTM that are considerably lower than those found for unfamiliar materials in traditional laboratory studies (e.g. Simon, 1976), which are often as high as 10s/item.

The structure of the acquired memory skill for digit span

In the digit-span task, subjects must reproduce all of the presented digits in the order they were shown. Subjects with exceptional digit-span per-

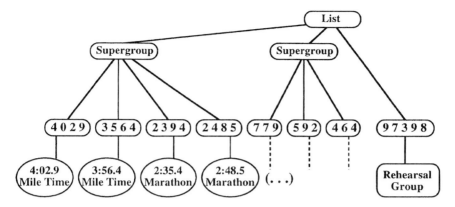

FIG. 6.1   An illustration of the memory representation of a list of 30 digits encoded with a retrieval structure similar to those used by one of Chase and Ericsson's (1981) digit span experts (SF). This retrieval structure has two supergroups, where each supergroup encodes the order of several digit groups. Each digit group is mnemonically encoded with encoding of categories or the types used by SF.

formance have been shown to meet these task demands by developing memory skills that share a common cognitive structure (Chase & Ericsson, 1981; 1982; Ericsson, 1985; 1988; Richman et al., 1995). Subjects break down the long presented sequences of digits into a series of digit groups, each of which typically contains either three or four digits (consistent with the limits of attention). As the digit groups are presented, they are encoded and stored in LTM using pre-existing knowledge about ages, dates, running times, and mathematics. For example, a subject might encode 4023 as a running time—in this case, perhaps interpreting it as 4 minutes, 2.3 seconds, which is a very good mile time. In addition, at the time of presentation the subjects associate each digit group with retrieval cues that uniquely specify the location of that group within the presented list of digits. At the time of recall, the subject regenerates the retrieval cues and uses them to access the associated digit groups, thus successfully recalling the complete list of digits in order.

The key acquired mechanism is the system of retrieval cues, referred to as the *retrieval structure*. Chase and Ericsson (1981; 1982) found that prior to each digit-span trial, subjects would rehearse the retrieval structure that contained information about how a given list would be segmented into a hierarchy of digit groups (see Fig. 6.1 for an illustration). During the presentation, subjects reported segmenting the sequences of digits according to the retrieval structure. They also reported using spatial retrieval cues to differentiate the encoding of digit groups at the lowest level (supergroups) of the hierarchy in Fig. 6.1. At the time of recall, pauses between successive digits were systematically related to the boundaries in their reported retrieval structure (Chase & Ericsson, 1981; Staszewski, 1988). Additional experimental studies involving cued recall (e.g. Chase & Ericsson, 1981; Staszewski, 1988) demonstrated that subjects had formed associations between digit groups and their corresponding locations in the retrieval structure. In a recent paper, Richman et al. (1995) implemented a computer model that was able to regenerate closely the observed performance of one of the trained subjects on the digit-span task. Although the assumptions of their model differ in significant ways from those of Chase and Ericsson (1982) and Ericsson and Kintsch (1995), the simulations by Richman et al. (1995) demonstrate the adequacy of a hierarchical retrieval structure to account for many aspects of the acquisition of vastly superior digit span.

Perhaps the best evidence for flexible recall based on retrieval structures is offered by the trained subjects' performance on the memorisation of digit matrices (illustrated in Fig. 6.2), which were originally used by Binet (1894) to study exceptional visual memory. Digit matrices consist of a 5-digit by 5-digit square arrangement of random digits (i.e. 25 digits total). The trained subjects (Ericsson & Chase, 1982) matched or surpassed the performance of Binet's (1894) exceptional subjects in the time required to memorise the matrix, and showed the same pattern of recall times for the different orders of recall (see Fig. 6.2 for three different examples). The recall times for both trained and "exceptional" subjects could be accounted for by an encoding of the matrix as five digit groups, each corresponding to a row—consistent with the trained subjects' verbal reports. The total time for each order of recall could be predicted by the number of times a new digit group (row of digits) had to be retrieved to complete the recall of the entire matrix. Recall of the matrix by row is relatively fast and involves only five time-consuming retrievals of different digit groups (see Fig. 6.2 for the steps). By contrast, recall by columns is slow, because it requires subjects to retrieve a different digit group for each of the 25 digits.

One problem with the repeated use of the same retrieval structure for memorising different digit lists within the same test session concerns the build-up of proactive interference (PI). Chase and Ericsson (1982) found considerable evidence for decrements in performance due to PI, and they and Staszewski (1990) found evidence for encoding methods where subjects tried to overcome problems with PI by elaborative encoding of relations among digit groups and among supergroups to supplement the generated associations with the retrieval structure, as illustrated in Fig. 6.3. These supplementary encodings correspond to generated structures in LTM that distinguish one list of digits from the previous ones. For example, a subject may notice that a supergroup consists of a pattern of mnemonic

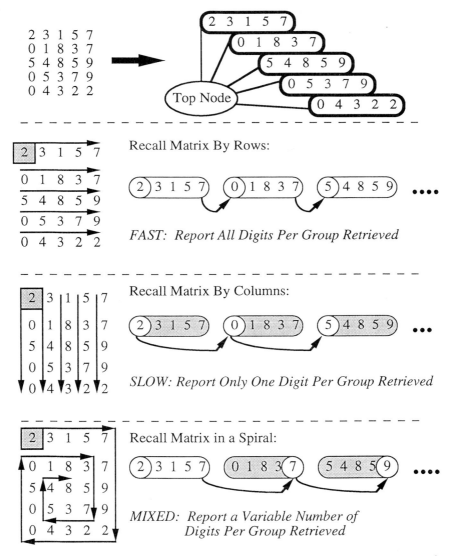

FIG. 6.2   Chase and Ericsson's (1982) digit-span experts were tested using matrices similar to that shown at the top. The experts memorised and encoded the matrix as five separate rows of digits in a retrieval structure (top). Three examples of different orders of recall used by Binet (1894) are shown in the left column. On the right side of each recall instruction the steps of retrieval are shown to recall the digits in the instructed order. The time-consuming step is to recall a new digit group (row of digits) from memory; once the relevant digit group is retrieved any digit within the digit group is rapidly accessed.

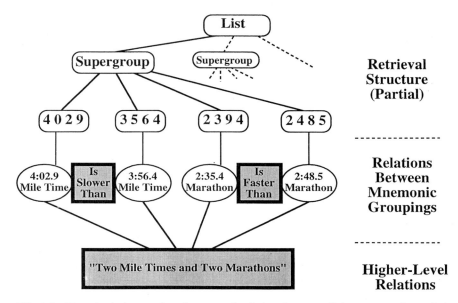

FIG. 6.3 Hypothetical examples of generated relations between digit groups and encoded patterns of mnemonic categories for the first supergroup in the retrieval structure shown in Fig. 6.1. These additional relations are stored in LTM, and facilitate recall of the most recent list of digits, as well as reducing the effects of proactive interference due to previous lists encoded with similar retrieval structures.

categories, such as two running times for a mile followed by two running times for the marathon. This encoded pattern would then be associated with the corresponding location in the retrieval structure (see Fig. 6.3) and would aid recall of the supergroup in the just-presented list of digits.

In summary, after only a few hundred hours of practice and training, subjects are able to attain a memory performance on the digit-span task that exceeds the typical performance by over 1000%. The acquired memory performance is mediated by rapid domain-specific encoding of digit groups in LTM, associations to acquired retrieval structures, and elaborative encodings generating new structures with relations among digit groups.

Ericsson and Kintsch (1995) have proposed that acquired retrieval structures and skills that generate integrated structures in LTM mediate the expanded working memory (LT-WM) of experts in their domain of expertise. According to their theory, experts acquire memory skills that combine the characteristics of these two types of general mechanisms to meet the retrieval and storage demands of working memory for tasks in their particular domain of expert performance. In the same fashion that experts in the digit-span task acquire retrieval structures for hierarchical encoding, experts in other domains will acquire memory skills that are uniquely adapted to the retrieval demands for LT-WM during performance in their domain.

WORKING MEMORY IN EXPERT PERFORMANCE

It is generally agreed that the superior performance of experts reflects the accumulation of domain-specific knowledge and the acquisition of effective strategies and skills to perform representative tasks in the corresponding domains of expertise. Ericsson and Kintsch's (1995) proposal for LT-WM simply suggests that attaining expert performance includes the acquisition of memory skills that allow experts selectively to store in LTM relevant information that must be kept accessible during subsequent processing. In this section, we will show that LT-WM provides a parsimonious account of experts' incidental memory for task-relevant information, their ability to continue processing after interruptions, and their superior memory for representative stimuli from their domain of expertise. In addition, we will discuss a few examples of expert performance and review evidence for how LT-WM is acquired and mediated by specific retrieval structures.

When experts are unexpectedly asked to recall information about a completed task the amount of accurate recall is often substantial and related to their level of expert performance. This has been shown in such diverse domains as chess, bridge, and medicine (Ericsson & Kintsch, 1995). This finding is consistent with the hypothesis that information is stored in LT-WM as a natural part of the experts' performance of domain-relevant tasks. However, the evidence for incidental recall does not by itself prove that the experts relied on the information in LTM to perform the task; it is still possible that storage in LTM was simply an indirect consequence of the task-relevant processing.

More compelling evidence for experts' reliance on LTM for temporary storage comes from studies where experts have been interrupted during processing and forced to engage in an unrelated attention-demanding task until information in ST-WM would no longer be accessible. If the information in working memory was restricted to that in ST-WM, then experts would be unable to continue processing. On the other hand, if experts were relying on storage in LT-WM, then they would only need to reinstate the retrieval cues that would make the stored information about the task accessible again, and allow the processing to continue. In their review, Ericsson and Kintsch (1995) found evidence for the latter, with the primary effects of disruptions consisting of additional time to reactivate relevant retrieval cues based on their general knowledge of the task and associated retrieval structure. Skills that allow experts to cope with distractions are necessary, because in most expert activities interruptions and social exchanges occur frequently. In some types of task, however, repeated use of a single retrieval structure is employed along with temporal cues and recency to maintain access to the most recent updates (e.g. mental calculation; Ericsson & Kintsch, 1995). In such cases, a disruption would have an effect by decreasing the temporal discriminability of the information stored in LT-WM.

The most distinctive phenomenon associated with expert performance concerns the vastly superior ability of experts to recall meaningful stimuli, but not randomly rearranged versions, after a brief exposure (see Ericsson and Lehmann, 1996, for a recent review of the extensive body of evidence from many different domains). Chase and Simon's (1973) original account of this phenomenon was based on the assumption that when exposures to stimuli were brief, storage was limited to ST-WM. They argued that the superior recall of experts was not due to storing a larger number of chunks in STM; instead, they proposed that each of the experts' chunks represented more complex chess patterns involving more chess pieces. For example, an expert chess player might recognise that a king, a rook and three pawns were in a castled-king position and maintain that familiar pattern as one chunk in ST-WM. Subsequent studies of briefly presented chess positions, however, showed that disruption of ST-WM prior to recall had essentially no impact, implying storage in LTM (Charness, 1976). Furthermore, the number of chunks recalled did not appear to be fixed, because Frey and Adesman (1976) found that skilled chess players could recall information from two consecutively presented chess positions almost as well as from a single position. More recently, Cooke, Atlas, Lane, and Berger (1993) and Gobet and Simon (1995) extended these findings, showing that highly skilled chess players can recall a substantial number of pieces from up to nine different chess positions presented at a comparable rapid rate. Hence, the superior memory performance of experts even for brief exposures involves storage in and recall from LT-WM.

The acquisition of LT-WM enables experts to maintain access to much more information using LTM than can be kept active in the limited-capacity ST-WM. At first sight, the acquisition of LT-WM might seem to eliminate any constraints on working-memory capacity. However, a closer analysis of specific instances of acquired memory skills in particular domains shows that the increased capacity is acquired slowly through deliberate practice. Furthermore, the increased capacity is specific to selected relevant information and is mediated by skills designed to enable rapid encoding and association of appropriate retrieval cues to assure efficient future retrieval. Therefore, the expanded working-memory capacity provided by LT-WM is domain-specific and its structure reflects an adaptation to the storage and retrieval demands of the corresponding task domain. In the following two sections, we will discuss the constraints on LT-WM in the context of particular domains, with special emphasis on its extended period of deliberate acquisition and its specific components as a function of task requirements.

The deliberate acquisition of superior working memory of experts

Across domains, exceptional performances of all types are more correlated with time spent in deliberate efforts to improve than with the amount of experience in activities within the domain (Charness, Krampe, & Mayr, 1996; Ericsson & Charness, 1994; Ericsson et al., 1993). Empirical findings on the acquisition of exceptional memory performance have found that memory skills are not an exception to this rule: merely possessing extensive experience in a domain need not lead to the use of retrieval structures or exceptional memory performance (Chase & Ericsson, 1981; Ericsson, 1985). Using retrieval structures to encode presented information requires the introduction of additional cognitive processes, and thus cannot be explained by automatisation of standard rehearsal by untrained subjects.

For instance, consider waiters and waitresses who memorise dinner orders for several customers at a time. Their encoding methods usually involve directly associating items from a particular customer's dinner order with an image of the corresponding customer. Optimal performance under these conditions is limited, because this technique creates considerable interference, owing to the high degree of similarity among the items involved. An exceptional waiter studied by Ericsson and Polson (1988a; 1988b), however, was found to be able to memorise up to 16 dinner orders without taking notes. Detailed analysis of his performance showed that he had acquired a unique set of encodings and a retrieval structure to perform the task. Consistent with requirements for practice, his memory performance improved gradually over years of practice.

The available results on the acquisition of experts' expanded working memory are similar. In Japan, students are very proficient in their use of an abacus to add large numbers rapidly. Some students are even able to add numbers using a mental abacus, but this ability is not a natural consequence of extensive training with a physical abacus. Hence, mental-abacus calculators need to practise extensively with mental problems (Stigler, 1984). After extended training, mental-abacus calculators are able to increase the number of digits that they can maintain mentally during the calculation. As a rule, one year of serious mental training is required for each additional digit (Hatano & Osawa, 1983). This increase in memory for digits is not associated with increased memory capacity for other types of materials (Hatano & Osawa, 1983).

Memory capacity for chess positions is closely related to chess skill, which generally increases as a function of years of serious chess playing. Recently, Charness et al. (1996) have shown that neither mere chess-playing experience nor amount of tournament play provides the best predictor of chess ratings, which presumably reflect skill, because they are based on wins and losses against other rated chess players. Instead, the most effective predictor of chess rating for a particular player is the accumulated amount of serious chess study alone or deliberate practice. Amount of chess playing does not predict chess skill once the amount of reported chess study is statistically controlled for. A typical activity in deliberate practice for chess involves the study of published games between chess masters, where the chess student's goal is to predict successfully each of the chess master's moves. Failure to predict a move forces the chess player to analyse the position more carefully by exploring the consequences of alternative move combinations through planning in an effort to uncover the reasons for the chess master's move. The depth of planning when selecting a move only increases with chess skill up to about the level of chess experts (Charness, 1981b; 1989; Saariluoma, 1990; 1992). However, the capacity to plan and mentally to represent chess positions still continues to increase with further chess skill, as shown by Saariluoma's (1991b) studies of blindfold chess. It is important to note that for skilled players, storage is not the only important issue; superior encoding and organisation of the chess position in memory are critical. The mental representation of the chess position must allow the chess master to identify promising moves and lines of play and support planning and evaluation. Research has shown that at the highest levels, superior chess skill is associated with rapid access to the best moves for a given position (de Groot, 1946/1978; Gobet & Simon, 1996; Saariluoma, 1990; 1992). In sum, superior memory for chess positions is not explicitly trained, but emerges as a consequence of very extended study activities involving planning and mental evaluations of chess positions.

Similarly, expert performance in medical diagnosis is acquired over many years of training. Although expert medical performance is often associated with increased memory for information about the patient, the principal superiority of medical experts concerns their selective encoding of relevant higher-level information to support reasoning about alternative diagnoses (see Ericsson and Kintsch, 1995, for a review). In many other types of expert performance as well, the critical aspect concerns selective extraction of relevant information and encoding of this information in a manner that facilitates retrieval during reasoning and planning (see Ericsson & Lehmann, 1996, for a review).

The structure of LT-WM as a consequence of informational demands

Given that LT-WM is an integrated aspect of expert performance, its specific structure will differ from domain to domain. The kinds of demands that various tasks place on memory differ greatly as a function of the complexity of the task. Because information must be actively and selectively encoded, we would expect to find that domains where the retrieval demands are clearly specified would produce relatively simple memory skills. More complex retrieval demands produce greater uncertainty about what needs to be encoded, leading to the use of more complex selection mechanisms and memory skills.

Some of the simplest and best-defined storage and retrieval demands are found in tasks that only require literal reproduction of presented information, such as the digit-span task discussed earlier. A skilled memoriser already knows how to encode the information for later recall at the time the information is presented. In this simple type of task, no decision about what information must be encoded need to be made, and the retrieval demands are known ahead of time. Reviews of research on expert memorists (Ericsson, 1988; Mahadevan, 1995) have confirmed that expert memory in memorists is typically associated with simple hierarchical elaborative encodings (Ericsson & Kintsch, 1995) and retrieval structures like those used by Chase and Ericsson's (1981; 1982) trained subjects.

Mental-calculation tasks, such as mental-multiplication and mental-abacus computation, are also well defined, as both are executed using stable computational strategies that dictate which information requires intermediate storage and which information must be retrieved at a later time. Although calculation tasks do require selective encoding of incoming information, it is possible to anticipate accurately the conditions of future recall.

Many skilled activities require more than a simple reproduction of presented items, however. Particularly in expert performance that involves working memory support for decision-making, planning, and reasoning, such as chess expertise, more complex mechanisms are required, which enable rapid access to meaningful clusters of information. Research on the selection of the best move for chess positions has found that the elite chess players perceive and meaningfully encode the configurations of chess pieces in the position rapidly and quickly access potential move sequences from LTM (de Groot, 1946/1978; Saariluoma, 1990). In fact, highly skilled chess players can often select very good chess moves even when the available decision time is dramatically reduced (Calderwood, Klein, & Crandall, 1988; Gobet & Simon, 1996). However, when elite chess players are allowed sufficient time systematically to evaluate alternative move sequences by planning, they can often discover superior "new" moves (de Groot, 1946/1978) and play at a higher level of chess skill (Gobet & Simon, 1996).

For effective planning, the memory representation must allow the expert to be able to represent mentally generated chess positions meaningfully and allow for evaluation of weaknesses and promising move sequences. At the same time the expert must have the ability to discover patterns and relations in the chess position that go beyond those already contained in the original encoding. In order to maximise the benefits of evaluation of mentally generated chess positions, experts need to be able to represent the positions in a format that allows generation and consideration of alternative interpretations. Ericsson and Oliver (Ericsson & Staszewski, 1989) proposed that chess experts have acquired a retrieval structure representing the 64 locations of a chessboard to supplement the meaningful encodings of the chess position. In support of this hypothesis, they found that a chess master could very rapidly retrieve information about the contents of individual locations and clusters of adjacent locations for a memorised chess position.

Recently, Saariluoma (1989) found that chess masters were able to commit a chess position to memory even when it was not all displayed at once in the traditional visual format. Instead, the position was presented as a sequential list of all individual pieces with their respective locations on the chess board. Under these conditions, chess masters were able to recall most of the information in regular chess positions as well as randomly arranged versions provided that the rate of presentation was sufficiently slow (around 4s/piece). In the beginning of this type of memory trial the location of the initially presented chess pieces must be encoded virtually exclusively by direct associations to the retrieval structure, as there are no opportunities for relational encodings with other chess pieces. Once more chess pieces have been presented then opportunities for relational encodings emerge. Even for random positions it is possible to discover meaningful relations between presented pieces that share spatial relations. In one of the experiments, Saariluoma (1989, Experiment 1) read the name and location of all the pieces from random and regular board configurations in an organised fashion. That is, rather than presenting the chess pieces and positions in a random order, he would, for example, present all the white pawns in succession from left to right, followed by the white king, queen, etc. He found that recall of both regular and random positions benefited from the organised presentation, although the benefit was greater for regular positions. This result suggests that subjects rely on relational encodings for both regular and random positions; but for regular chess positions, larger and better-integrated patterns of chess pieces are also retrieved to facilitate a hierarchical integration of the encoding of the position in LTM. In support of that hypothesis, Saariluoma (1989, Experiment 3) found that when chess masters were presented with several chessboard arrangements in sequence, they were unable to maintain more than one random position, but could recall several regular chess positions. The maintenance of encoded relations between pieces and locations in a random position therefore appear to depend critically on the retrieval structure, which can only uniquely index a single chessboard arrangement at a time. Regular chess positions, however, can be encoded as meaningfully organised entire chess positions stored in LTM, and thus do not depend on the retrieval structure to maintain access to lower-level patterns.

Selection of relevant information for encoding in LT-WM is not a critical issue for the very best chess players, because the locations of all of the chess pieces are potentially pertinent to the selection of a move for a given chess position. Consistent with this claim, chess players' memory performance increases monotonically with chess skill, as noted earlier. By contrast, selection and appropriate encoding of relevant information is critical to expert performance in many other domains of expertise. Studies of medical experts show that with increasing expertise a higher-level representation of disease aspects relevant to medical diagnosis is acquired (see Ericsson & Kintsch, 1995; and Patel, Arocha, & Kaufmann, 1994, for reviews). This representation allows the experts selectively to identify and to encode these aspects rather than maintaining many specific isolated facts about the patient in working memory. The aspects are carefully developed to reflect general characteristics independent of particular diagnoses and allow the expert to accumulate information in LT-WM that can support decision-making and reasoning about many different diagnostic possibilities without any need to reinterpret the original facts about the patient. In this higher-level expert representation many specific facts about the patient are not retained, which can explain why memory performance for all types of facts about patients does not increase monotonically with expert performance in medical diagnosis (Patel & Groen, 1991; Schmidt & Boshuizen, 1993). In medical expertise and many other types of expert performance, mere capacity to reproduce presented information is not essential. Instead, the critical aspect of LT-WM concerns acquired representations that assure accessibility to the vast integrated body of relevant knowledge within the domain (Glaser & Chi, 1988), and allow effective reasoning and evaluation about available options.

In summary, LT-WM is an integrated aspect of expert performance that is developed to meet the special demands of increased working memory for that particular activity. Many years of deliberate practice are typically required to attain the necessary encoding methods and retrieval structure.

Viewing the superior memory of experts as acquired skills to support performance provides a framework for accounting for superior domain-specific memory performance as well as several instances where experts' memory performance for domain-specific information is not reliably superior to novices' (Ericsson & Lehmann, 1996).

GENERAL DISCUSSION AND BROADER IMPLICATIONS

In this chapter, we have reviewed empirical evidence showing that experts' working memory is not restricted to transiently activated information (ST-WM). Rapid storage of new information in LTM that is mediated by task-specific memory skills (LT-WM) is the most important factor. The recently stored information is kept accessible by associated retrieval cues in ST-WM. This proposal for LT-WM (Ericsson & Kintsch, 1995) is consistent with the massive body of laboratory studies documenting that, for unfamiliar materials and tasks, storage in LTM is slow and unreliable, because LT-WM is mediated by memory skills that require extensive practice to develop. Whereas the typical laboratory research in memory has focused on domain-general characteristics of human memory, the proposal for LT-WM shows how the functional domain-specific capacity of working memory can be increased by acquired knowledge, strategies, and memory skills. The primary implication of LT-WM is that the functional capacity of working-memory and storage characteristics of LTM are not invariably fixed across all domains. Instead, they can be modified through the acquisition of domain-specific support skills in a fashion similar to that of skills of other types.

The focus of our chapter has been on the highest levels of expert performance, where the evidence for LT-WM is the most striking. However, increases in working-memory capacity and LT-WM are observed as a function of increases in level of performance during the extended period of acquisition of expert performance as well. Hence, one would expect that expansion of working-memory capacity through acquisition of LT-WM is possible and even likely in any skilled cognitive activity with heavy demands on working memory. Some of the best empirical evidence for this hypothesis is found in the area of text comprehension. It is well known that subjects have substantial incidental memory for text and can answer comprehension questions after reading. More interestingly, Glanzer and colleagues (for a review, see Glanzer & Nolan, 1986) have shown that interrupting subjects in the middle of reading a text with 30 seconds of an unrelated activity does not impair comprehension of the text. The only consequence of the disruption is that subjects require slightly longer reading times on the first sentence after the interruption. Ericsson and

Kintsch (1995) showed that these and other findings are consistent with successive storage and updates of an integrated representation of the text in LTM, where the increased reading times after the interruption reflect the necessary time to reinstate in ST-WM the retrieval cues needed to access the LTM-based representation of the text.

They also reviewed evidence that individual differences in working memory capacity during reading do not reflect innate, fixed capacity differences, in contrast with traditional theories (Just & Carpenter, 1992; Daneman & Carpenter, 1980). Instead, such individual capacity differences primarily reflect differences in the relevant knowledge and acquired memory skills that support encoding of the text in LT-WM. It is likely that many other everyday mental skills, such as decision-making, planning, and problem-solving can be fully understood once the memory skills supporting working memory are given equal consideration with other aspects of these acquired skills.

ACKNOWLEDGEMENT

We would like to thank Andreas C. Lehmann for his helpful comments on an earlier draft of this manuscript.

REFERENCES

Anderson, J.R. (1982). Acquisition of cognitive skill, *Psychological Review, 89*, 369–406.

Anderson, J.R. (1983). *The architecture of cognition.* Cambridge, MA: Harvard University Press.

Atkinson, R.C., & Shiffrin, R.M. (1968). Human memory: A proposed system and its control processes. In K. Spence & J. Spence (Eds.), *The psychology of learning and motivation* (Vol. 2, pp. 89–195). New York: Academic Press.

Atwood, M.E., & Polson, P.G. (1976). A process model for water jug problems. *Cognitive Psychology, 8*, 191–216.

Binet, A. (1894). *Psychologie des grands calculateurs et joueurs d'echecs* ['The psychology of great calculators and chess players']. Paris: Librairie Hachette.

Broadbent, D.E. (1975). The magic number seven after fifteen years. In A. Kennedy & A. Wilkes (Eds.), *Studies in long-term memory* (pp. 3–18). London: Wiley.

Calderwood, R., Klein, G.A., & Crandall, B.W. (1988). Time pressure, skill and move quality in chess. *American Journal of Psychology, 101*, 481–493.

Chaiken, S.R. (1994). The inspection time not studied: Processing speed ability unrelated to psychometric intelligence. *Intelligence, 19*, 295–316.

Charness, N. (1976). Memory for chess positions: Resistance to interference. *Journal of Experimental Psychology: Human Learning and Memory, 2*, 641–653.

Charness, N. (1981a). Ageing and skilled problem solving. *Journal of Experimental Psychology: General, 110*, 21–38.

Charness, N. (1981b). Search in chess: Age and skill differences. *Journal of Experimental Psychology: Human Perception and Performance, 7*, 467–476.

Charness, N. (1989). Expertise in chess and bridge. In D. Klahr & K. Kotovsky (Eds.), *Complex information processing: The impact of Herbert A. Simon* (pp. 183–208). Hillsdale, NJ: Lawrence Erlbaum Associates Inc.

Charness, N., Krampe, R. Th., & Mayr, U. (1996). The role of practice and coaching in entrepreneurial skill domains: An international comparison of life-span chess skill acquisition. In K.A. Ericsson (Ed.), *The road to excellence: The acquisition of expert performance in the arts and sciences, sports, and games* (pp. 51–80). Mahweh, NJ: Erlbaum.

Chase, W.G., & Ericsson, K.A. (1981). Skilled memory. In J.R. Anderson (Ed.), *Cognitive skills and their acquisition* (pp. 141–189). Hillsdale, NJ: Lawrence Erlbaum Associates Inc.

Chase, W. G. & Ericsson, K. A. (1982). Skill and working memory. In G.H. Bower (Ed.), *The psychology of learning and motivation* (Vol. 16, pp. 1–58). New York: Academic Press.

Chase, W.G., & Simon, H.A. (1973). The mind's eye in chess. In W.G. Chase (Ed.), *Visual information processing* (pp. 215–281). New York: Academic Press.

Cooke, N.J., Atlas, R.S., Lane, D.M., & Berger, R.C. (1993). Role of high-level knowledge in memory for chess positions. *American Journal of Psychology, 106,* 321–351.

de Groot, A. (1978). *Thought and choice in chess.* The Hague, Netherlands: Mouton. (Original work published 1946.)

Daneman, M., & Carpenter, P.A. (1980). Individual differences in working memory and reading. *Journal of Verbal Learning and Verbal Behavior, 19,* 450–466.

Ebbinghaus, H. (1964). *Memory: A contribution to experimental psychology* (H.A. Ruger & C.E. Bussenius, Trans.). New York: Dover Publications. (Original work published 1885.)

Ericsson, K.A. (1985). Memory skill. *Canadian Journal of Psychology, 39,* 188–231.

Ericsson, K.A. (1988). Analysis of memory performance in terms of memory skill. In R.J. Sternberg (Ed.), *Advances in the psychology of human intelligence* (Vol. 4, pp. 137–179). Hillsdale, NJ: Lawrence Erlbaum Associates Inc.

Ericsson, K.A., & Charness, N. (1994). Expert performance: Its structure and acquisition. *American Psychologist, 49,* 725–747.

Ericsson, K.A., & Chase, W.G. (1982). Exceptional memory. *American Scientist, 70,* 607–615.

Ericsson, K.A., Chase, W.G., & Faloon, S. (1980). Acquisition of a memory skill. *Science, 208,* 1181–1182.

Ericsson, K.A., & Kintsch, W. (1995). Long-term working memory. *Psychological Review, 102,* 211–245.

Ericsson, K.A., Krampe, R. Th., & Tesch-Römer, C. (1993). The role of deliberate practice in the acquisition of expert performance. *Psychological Review, 100(3),* 363–406.

Ericsson, K.A., & Lehmann, A.C. (1996). Expert and exceptional performance: Evidence on maximal adaptations on task constraints. *Annual Review of Psychology, 47,* 273–305.

Ericsson, K.A., & Polson, P.G. (1988a). Memory for restaurant orders. In M. T. H. Chi, R. Glaser, & M. Farr (Eds.), *The nature of expertise* (pp. 23–70). Hillsdale, NJ: Lawrence Erlbaum Associates Inc.

Ericsson, K.A., & Polson, P.G. (1988b). Experimental analysis of the mechanisms of a memory skill. *Journal of Experimental Psychology: Learning, Memory and Cognition, 14,* 305–316.

Ericsson, K.A., & Staszewski, J. (1989). Skilled memory and expertise: Mechanisms of exceptional performance. In D. Klahr & K. Kotovsky (Eds.), *Complex information processing: The impact of Herbert A. Simon* (pp. 235–267). Hillsdale, NJ: Lawrence Erlbaum Associates Inc.

Fitts, P., & Posner, M.I. (1967). *Human performance.* Belmont, CA: Brooks/Cole.

Frey, P.W., & Adesman, P. (1976). Recall memory for visually presented chess positions. *Memory and Cognition, 4,* 541–547.

Glanzer, M., & Nolan, S.D. (1986). Memory mechanisms in text comprehension. In G.H. Bower (Ed.), *The psychology of learning and motivation* (pp. 275–317). New York: Academic Press.

Glaser, R., & Chi, M.T.H. (1988). Overview. In M.T.H. Chi, R. Glaser & M.J. Farr (Eds.), *The nature of expertise* (pp. xv–xxviii). Hillsdale, NJ: Lawrence Erlbaum Associates Inc.

Gobet, F., & Simon, H.A. (1995). Templates in chess memory: A mechanism for recalling several boards. *Complex Information Processes, working paper #513*. Pittsburgh, PA: Carnegie Mellon University.

Gobet, F., & Simon, H.A. (1996). The roles of recognition processes and look-ahead search in time-constrained expert problem solving: Evidence from grandmaster level chess. *Psychological Science, 7*, 52–55.

Hatano, G., & Osawa, K. (1983). Digit memory of grand experts in abacus-derived mental calculation. *Cognition, 15*, 95–110.

Holding, D.H. (1985). *The psychology of chess skill*, Hillsdale, NJ: Lawrence Erlbaum Associates Inc.

Jensen, A.R. (1990). Speed of information processing in a calculating prodigy. *Intelligence, 14*, 259–274.

Just, M.A., & Carpenter, P.A. (1992). A capacity theory of comprehension. *Psychological Review, 99*, 122–149.

Koltanowski, G. (1985). *In the dark*. Coraopolis, PA: Chess Enterprises.

Lane, D.M., & Robertson, L. (1979). The generality of levels of processing hypothesis: An application to memory for chess positions. *Memory and Cognition, 7*, 253–256.

Levine, M. (1966). Hypothesis behavior by humans during discrimination learning. *Journal of Experimental Psychology, 71*, 331–338.

Mahadevan, R.S. (1995). *Exceptional memory: Deviation to normal memory laws?* Specialty paper. Department of Psychology, Florida State University, Tallahassee.

Miller, G.A. (1956). The magical number seven, plus or minus two: Some limits of our capacity for processing information. *Psychological Review, 63*, 81–97.

Newell, A. (1990). *Unified theories of cognition*. Cambridge, MA: Harvard University Press.

Newell, A., & Simon, H.A. (1972). *Human problem solving*. Englewood Cliffs, NJ: Prentice-Hall.

Norman, G.R., Brooks, L.R., & Allen, S.W. (1989). Recall by expert medical practitioners and novices as a record of processing attention. *Journal of Experimental Psychology: Learning, Memory and Cognition, 15*, 1166–1174.

Patel, V.L., Arocha, J.F., & Kaufmann, D.R. (1994). Diagnostic reasoning and medical expertise. *The Psychology of Learning and Motivation, 30*, 187–251.

Patel, V.L., & Groen, G.J. (1991). The general and specific nature of medical expertise: A critical look. In K.A. Ericsson & J. Smith (Eds.), *Toward a general theory of expertise* (pp. 93–125). Cambridge, MA: Cambridge University Press.

Payne, J.W. (1976). Task complexity and contingent processing in decision making: An informational search and protocol analysis. *Organizational Behavior and Human Performance, 16*, 366–387.

Richman, H., Staszewski, J.J., & Simon, H.A. (1995). Simulation of expert memory using EPAM IV. *Psychological Review, 102*, 305–330.

Saariluoma, P. (1989). Chess players' recall of auditorily presented chess positions. *European Journal of Cognitive Psychology, 1*, 309–320.

Saariluoma, P. (1990). Apperception and restructuring in chess players' problem solving. In K.J. Gilhooly, M.T.G. Keene, R.H. Logie, & G. Erdos (Eds.), *Lines of thought: Reflections on the psychology of thinking* (Vol. 2, pp. 41–57). London: Wiley.

Saariluoma, P. (1991a). Visuo-spatial interference and apperception in chess. In R.H. Logie and M. Denis (Eds.), *Mental images in human cognition* (pp. 83–94). Amsterdam: Elsevier Science Publishers.

Saariluoma, P. (1991b). Aspects of skilled imagery in blindfold chess. *Acta Psychologica, 77*, 65–89.

Saariluoma, P.G. (1992). Error in chess: The apperception restructuring view. *Psychological Research, 54,* 17–26.

Schmidt, H.G., & Boshuizen, H.P.A. (1993). On the origin of intermediate effects in clinical case recall. *Memory and Cognition, 21,* 338–351.

Simon, H.A. (1976). The information-storage system called "human memory". In M.R. Rosenzweig & E.L. Bennett (Eds.), *Neural mechanisms of learning and memory* (pp. 79–96). Cambridge, MA: MIT Press.

Smith, S.B. (1983). *The great mental calculators.* New York: Columbia University Press.

Staszewski, J.J. (1988). The psychological reality of retrieval structures: An investigation of expert knowledge (doctoral dissertation, Cornell University, 1987). *Dissertation Abstracts International, 48,* 2126B.

Staszewski, J.J. (1990). Exceptional memory: The influence of practice and knowledge on development of elaborative encoding strategies. In W. [Wolfgang] Schneider & F. Weinert (Eds.), *Interactions among aptitudes, strategies, and knowledge in cognitive performance* (pp. 252–285). New York: Springer Verlag.

Stigler, J.W. (1984). "Mental abacus": The effect of abacus training on Chinese children's mental calculation *Cognitive Psychology, 16,* 145–176.

CHAPTER SEVEN

Adversary Problem-solving and Working Memory

Pertti Saariluoma
University of Helsinki, Finland

TASK ANALYSIS

The term "adversary problem-solving" is normally used to describe situations in which two or more opponents are trying to achieve some goal (Gilhooly, 1989; Nilsson, 1971). The passive or defensive side tries to prevent the active or attacking side from doing so. This kind of problem-solving usually appears in situations of human conflict and competition. Adversary situations are common in games and sports, but they may also occur in many fields of practical life. It is not only chess and tennis that constitute adversary situations; business life, politics, courtrooms, diplomacy, and military actions also provoke them (Amsel, Langer & Loutzenhisher, 1991; Voss, Wolfe, Lawrence, & Engle, 1991; Wagner, 1991). Even some apparently one-party situations such as science or medicine may sometimes be interpreted as a game against nature, and thus they may share psychological properties with genuine adversary situations (Simon 1977). Hintikka's game-theoretical semantics serves as a very non-standard example of an adversary interpretation of an apparently very clearly non-adversary situation, i.e. the determination of sentence meanings (e.g. Hintikka & Kulas, 1983).

Game theory and some of its close derivatives such as state-space search constitute the standard formalisations of adversary problem-solving situations (Jones, 1980; von Neumann & Morgenstern, 1944; Newell & Simon, 1972). All the parties have a number of operations, e.g. investment opportunities, at their disposal in such situations. These operations change the total situation from one state to another. Transformation sequences from an initial state are normally best described as a tree (von Neumann and Morgenstern, 1944; Newell & Simon, 1972). This tree is ordinarily called the problem-space (Newell & Simon, 1972).

Though mathematically very satisfactory, game-theoretical explications of adversary problem-solving situations provide psychology with only a formal framework for considering the logic of a total situation. Game theory is far too abstract a conceptualisation directly to provide psychology with sufficiently expressive theoretical notions. In a normal adversary problem-solving situation, which can be met in business or politics, people are not able to examine exhaustively all the possibilities. This means that operation selection is always necessary.

The crucial role of operation selection can be made concrete with an example from chess. While current computers search for millions of positions a second, people hardly ever generate more than a hundred. None the less, the best human chess players are still as good as the best computer programs (de Groot, 1965; 1966; Hsu, Anantharaman, Campell, & Nowatzyk, 1990; Newell & Simon, 1972). Hence, for those who are interested in the human mind and the human way of thinking, it is crucial to understand how selectivity in human thinking is possible. It is not the game-theoretical logic, but the psychological preconditions of operation selection that are crucial from the psychological point of view.

The classic solutions to problems of operation selection were based on heuristic search (Holding, 1985; Newell & Simon, 1972). In this mathematically justified model, problem-solvers generate all the alternative operations to the depth of one or more, and then a heuristic evaluation function determines which of the generated operation sequences is the most advantageous. The search continued from that state onwards. Although this model operates excellently in computer programs, it has very little realism where human thinking is concerned. It is probabilistic, and in most task-environments the generation of all possibilities even to the depth of one "move" is unrealistic. In making an investment decision, for example, one cannot normally generate all imaginable ways to invest and heuristically select the best: There simply exist all too many ways to make the decision. This is why heuristic-search models are too coarse to be realistic models of the mind. Much more sophisticated analysis is required in order to explain human problem-solving behaviour (Chase & Simon, 1973).

HUMAN ERROR IN ADVERSARY PROBLEM-SOLVING

Human behaviour in adversary situations is problem-solving behaviour, because problem-solving processes appear when human beings do not have any immediate means to decide what to do, and operation selection is a non-trivial mental task (Dewey, 1910; Newell & Simon, 1972). However, the importance of errors in adversary problem-solving situations gives a very specific character to the problem-solving analysis. Nevertheless, the function of errors has scarcely begun to be analysed (Simon, 1974b).

Any human action with a certain intention, but which does not lead to the intended goal, can be called human error (Reason, 1990). In considering both the conceptual structure of adversary situations and human behaviour in such situations, errors are of paramount importance, because this apparently simple concept enables psychologists to connect human mental processes with the logical structure of adversary situations. Human errors explain why adversary processes may, in the long run, have certain outcomes. In the following analysis of the role of errors, which explicates some ideas that are more or less intuitively known by chess players, for example, the intention is to develop a connection between errors and the psychological study of thinking (see Reti, 1933).

It is assumed that an adversary problem-solving situation is one of balance between opponents. It can thus be postulated for all such situations that victory for one side can be achieved only if the other side makes an error. This conclusion is a trivial consequence of the notion of balance, but it has surprisingly important consequences for the psychological analysis of adversary problem-solving situations.

The thesis that victory in a balanced situation can be achieved only by virtue of errors can be inferred from the very notion of a balanced situation. A situation is balanced when both parties have chances of equalling each other's operations; otherwise, the situation is unbalanced, and one of the parties is superior. Consequently, in a balanced situation, the only means of shaking the equilibrium is for one of the parties not to counteract an operation of the opponent with an operation of similar weight. This kind of reaction can be called an error, because the party that makes the error has not been able to achieve its intention. Because, in balanced situations, all parties must always have access to operations of similar weight, errors are the only explanation of why the balance changes to the detriment of one of the parties. Thus errors and their psychological preconditions constitute the very core of any psychological considerations of adversary problem-solving.

Although the notion of balance is central in the aforementioned considerations, the logic does not essentially change if the situation is unbalanced. For definition, an adversary problem-solving situation is unbalanced if both parties are not able to carry out equally effective operations. Therefore, an unbalanced situation can be transformed into a balanced one, only if the party with the upper hand is unable to find the best choice, and thus loses its superiority. Naturally, losing superiority is an error. On the other hand, errors may also make an unbalanced situation even worse for the weaker party (cf. Simon, 1974b). Surprisingly, good operations are not directly decisive, because they can, in principle, always be matched by equally good operations. Thus only errors may shake the balance, and reaching the goal is possible only if the opponent is unable to maintain the balance.

The loss of balance depends on errors, and some errors may be more serious than others. Losing a pawn or £1 million is a less serious error than losing a queen or £100 million. The reason for the different consequences of errors is that coming back is much more difficult after some errors than after others. The greater the superiority of one side after an error, the less chance the inferior side has of bouncing back: The capture of a bishop does not in itself compensate for the loss of a queen, although it does compensate for the loss of a pawn.

The importance of errors in the structure of adversary situations makes it rational to consider the psychological problems of adversary situations in the light of human errors. This is why the main psychological problem in adversary problem-solving situations may be seen in the empirical and theoretical explication of the psychological preconditions of human errors. Such an explication requires, among many other issues, an understanding of the role of working memory in the occurrence of thought errors.

PROBLEM-SOLVING IN ADVERSARY SITUATIONS

Adversary problem-solving is necessarily content-specific, because human thinking must have some content. This is why empirical analysis of any thought process must incorporate a concrete task environment (Hunt, 1991). The following empirical analysis strongly relies on evidence collected in studying the psychology of chess players' problem-solving. The reason for this is simple. Chess has been, and to some extent still is, at the forefront of adversary problem-solving research. It just happens to be a well-defined task environment, which nevertheless provides information about complex problem-solving processes, and this is why it has been used for decades as the fruitfly of thought psychology (Charness, 1992; de Groot, 1965; 1966; Holding, 1985; 1992; Newell & Simon, 1972; Saariluoma, 1995). Chess research provides very good empirical evidence on some issues, including the relation of memory and problem-solving, which has very seldom, if at all, been researched in other task environments.

Research into chess players' problem-solving has demonstrated that they abstract small problem subspaces searchable by humans, which they manipulate in searching for effective solutions (Saariluoma, 1990; 1992b, in press). These subspaces can be called mental spaces. Mental-space abstraction is the way selective thinking operates in chess, but, undoubtedly, chess players' problem-solving provides much more general information about operations' selection process in thinking. Chess players' mental-space abstraction may be considered an example of the classic psychological process of *apperception*, and understanding this process would undoubtedly increase our understanding of the selectivity that gives human thinking its specific character (Kant, 1781; Leibniz, 1704/1979; Saariluoma, 1990; 1992a, in press; Stout, 1896; Wundt, 1880).

Mental-space abstraction is a highly conceptual process and in chess, for example, the contents of mental spaces are not equivalent to the contents of physically perceivable information. The pieces in chess players' mental spaces are located very differently from the real physically perceivable pieces on the chessboard. In fact, the physical locations can be seen by all, but only very good chess players can construct really rational mental spaces with highly functional and self-consistent contents (Saariluoma, 1990, in press). Moreover, the construction of mental spaces mostly relies on mental images (Saariluoma, 1992b).

The conceptual character of mental spaces is particularly clear in terms of cognitive structure. The elements of these representations are selected not on perceptual but on content-specific grounds. In chess, attack, defence, blockade, escape, and some other functional and content-specific principles effectively explain precisely why those moves are included in a particular mental space, while so many possibilities are eliminated. Furthermore, the same principles explain why, in the same position, some moves are relevant in one mental space but irrelevant in many alternative spaces. This content-specificity of chess players' mental spaces makes it groundless and super-ficial to explain mental-space abstraction in terms of perceptual processing (Saariluoma, 1990; 1992b; 1995; see Allport, 1980, for an alternative interpretation of content-specificity).

Discrepancy between the contents of physically perceivable information and mental representations can be derived in any area of expertise, and indeed between practically any precept and mental representation. The mental representations of diplomats in world crises or business managers concerning the future consequences of investments are necessarily independent of the stimulus information offered by their physical environment (cf. Voss, Wolfe, Lawrence, & Engle, 1991; Wagner, 1991). Missiles and markets are not perceivable, and even if they were, the percepts have very little use to contribute to the mental representations of diplomats or managers. Only highly selected and meaningful perceptual messages, such as opponents' suggestions and demands or market statistics, may contribute. Even then, perceptual analysis cannot determine why these pieces of information are relevant. Moreover, percepts always contain much more information than is mentally represented. The information available in a glimpse, and the information relevant in any action, share only a few environmental details.

Apperception and perception thus differ; firstly, because perception is stimulus-bound, but the contents of apperceived representations need not be temporally or spatially related to the contents of the physical stimulus environment. Secondly, the focus of apperception cannot be understood in perceptual terms only. It is because of this general discrepancy between physically perceivable and actually represented information contents that the process of abstracting mental spaces and other problem representations should be studied as an apperceptive rather than as a perceptual process (Saariluoma 1990; 1992; 1995).

The decisive stage in all adversary problem-solving is thus apperceptive problem subspace abstraction. The party that is able to apperceive mental spaces with more rational and truthful contents will, *ceteris paribus*, win. Of course, chance or luck may play a part in accidental situations with uncertain consequences, but, in the long run, any reliance on good luck is doomed to failure.

THE MAIN FUNCTIONAL CHARACTERISTICS OF WORKING MEMORY

Apperceiving mental contents is the core of human thinking (Leibniz, 1704/1979). However, neither apperceptive abstraction nor thinking can take place in a "vacuum". The abstracted mental contents must be stored somewhere in the human information-processing system, because otherwise these mental contents could not exist. This argument is obvious in terms of the classic theory of signs. Information only exists in the form of signs, but a sign, or any piece of information, can exist only if it has a material basis termed a sign vehicle (Morris, 1938). Of course, memory can serve in cognitive psychology as a mediating theoretical concept, which can express the functions of a sign vehicle for thoughts, thus saving researchers from having to go directly to neural concepts. All thoughts must be represented in memory. Thus memory systems are an essential component of the psychology of human problem-solving. It is not only the laws of content-specific information integration, but also those of memory that must be used in understanding and explaining psychological phenomena related to the human problem-solving process (Saariluoma, 1995).

Three attributes of memory systems, all related to working memory, are particularly important in human problem-solving research. The first is the limited information-storage capacity of the working memory, the second is its modular structure, and the third the collaboration of working memory with long-term memory. All these attributes are manifestly properties of working memory, because this is the system in which most of the active information manipulation takes place (Anderson, 1983; Baddeley, 1986; Baddeley & Hitch, 1974). This active nature of working memory explains why it is so important to use its methods and concepts in the research into adversary problem-solving.

WORKING MEMORY CAPACITY AND HUMAN ERRORS

It has consistently been shown that working-memory capacity sets limits on human thinking. It has been known since the mid-1950s that human working memory can keep only a very limited amount of information unless it is well chunked (Miller, 1956; Simon, 1974a; Watkins, 1977). Later, expertise research revealed that chunking is the essence of human expertise, and research into human thinking showed that working-memory capacity explains various kinds of thought errors (Chase & Simon, 1973).

Skilled chess players are able to recall chess positions better than novices (Chase & Simon, 1973; Djakov, Petrovsky, & Rudik, 1926; de Groot, 1965; 1966). When positions were randomised and the presentation time was short, viz. about 10 seconds, experts were no longer superior to novices (Chase & Simon, 1973). Because expert superiority could be explained in terms of chunking, it was natural to think that chess players would store the chess-specific information for their ongoing problem-solving process in their working memories. Working memory was also correctly thought to be a major bottleneck in chess players' information-processing.

The limited processing capacity of human working memory was very soon understood to be an important factor in several different fields of expertise from bridge to computing (for reviews, see Charness, 1992; Saariluoma, 1994; 1995). It was shown to be the case that working-memory limits prevented novices from master-level achievements. Novices simply could not construct sufficiently complex representations when this was necessary, i.e. representations of all the details that were representable by masters (Charness, 1981a; 1981b; Chase & Simon, 1973; Holding, 1985; Saariluoma, 1992a).

Finally, in the 1980s, it was realised that systematic errors appeared in thinking when people had to represent more information than their limited-capacity working memory could store (Anderson & Jeffries, 1985; Johnson-Laird, 1983; Johnson-Laird & Byrne, 1991; Reason, 1990). In problem-solving, decision-making, and reasoning research, increasing task complexity made thought processes substantially more difficult, and experts were normally shown to be able to generate more complex solutions when required (Charness, 1981a; 1981b; Jungermann, 1983; Montgomery & Svensson, 1976).

The consistency of the evidence connecting working-memory capacity with thinking is clear, and it means that any attempt to consider thought errors in adversary problem-solving situations must account for working-memory lapses. When the complexity of a task surpasses the storage capacity of the problem-solver, the risk of failure is apparent. This fact calls attention to the complexity of the environment and the required mental representations (Reason, 1990).

THE FUNCTIONS OF SUBSYSTEMS

The function of working-memory subsystems is the next important aspect of working memory that must be taken into account when discussing thought errors. Research into articulatory and visuo-spatial working memory has actually brought the problems of modularity into the psychology of thinking. Modularity in human information-processing was introduced as a concept and as a phenomenon in the early 1970s. Allport, Antonis, and Reynolds (1972) demonstrated the existence of modular subsystems in attention, and, at around the same time, Baddeley and Hitch (1974) presented their successful model of modular working memory (Baddeley, 1986; 1992). Nevertheless, modularity problems have not been sufficiently clearly recognised in literature on thinking (for the few exceptions see, e.g. Gilhooly, Logie, Wetherick, & Wynn, 1993; Hitch, 1978; Logie, Gilhooly, & Wynn, 1994; Logie & Salaway, 1990).

Specifically, in adversary problem-solving literature, the main evidence for the relevance of modularity in thinking comes from analyses of chess players' thinking (Baddeley, 1992; Bradley, Hudson, Robbins, & Baddeley, 1987; Holding, 1989; Saariluoma, 1991b; 1992a; 1992b). This research has systematically implied that short-term working memory has very special functions in human thinking, and these are related to information manipulation and transformation.

When chess players have to carry out visuo-spatial secondary tasks their processing is clearly impaired, although practically no effect can be found with articulatory secondary tasks. This asymmetry between the working-memory "slave systems" has been demonstrated in a number of primary tasks. Bradley et al. (1987) showed the asymmetry in recall experiments and Saariluoma, 1991b; 1992a; 1992b) in information intake and problem-solving tasks.

The empirical evidence thus suggests strongly that chess players mainly use their visuo-spatial memory when searching for a new move. Further evidence has been found in blindfold chess tasks, in which information is provided auditorily. Again, it is the visuo-spatial and not the articulatory tasks that impair the level of performance (Saariluoma, 1992b). Clearly, representational modality is decisive, and input modality of secondary value, in chess players' thinking. Input information is used to construct mental space, and this is manipulated and transformed in working memory.

Chess players construct relevant mental spaces in their visuo-spatial working memory for temporary manipulation using operations akin to mental transformation (Bundesen & Larsen, 1975; Chase & Simon, 1973; Cooper & Shepard, 1973). They thus use their visuo-spatial working memory for simulating reality, which is common in human thinking (cf. Denis, 1991). Of course, chess is a highly visuo-spatial task, and it is pointless to claim that all adversary problem-solving utilises visuo-spatial working memory. Though not adversary problem-solving, Hitch's (1978) research on mental arithmetic, for example, provides an alternative pattern of results. On the other hand, some results are in line with those concerning chess. Logie and Salaway (1990), for example, have shown that mental transformation is impaired by visuo-spatial secondary tasks. This suggests that, in thinking, working memory allocates processing among the subsystems depending on the nature of the task environment. However, the claim that working subsystems are systematically used to simulate reality, spatial and non-spatial, seems fairly credible.

The outcome of the experiments referred to demonstrates a new source of thought errors, which may be explained in terms of working memory. This is the dual use of one subsystem. Baddeley (1986) provides a concrete real-life example of what may happen by revealing how imagining an American football game interfered with his car driving. Without proper concentration, dual use of one of the working-memory subsystems may easily appear in practical life. This is why psychologists attempting to diagnose thought errors should be alert to the dual use of working-memory subsystems.

APPERCEPTIVE ERRORS AND WORKING MEMORY: SPECULATIONS ON THE ROLE OF CENTRAL EXECUTIVE

Working-memory and subsystem overload are not the sole source of thought errors. When chess players, for example, make numerous errors, the solutions for which would only require encoding one single move, memory overload can hardly be the sole explanation (Saariluoma, 1992b). These kinds of errors can be called apperceptive errors and may arise because subjects encode suboptimal or incorrect mental spaces without being able to recover from their illusory representations (Saariluoma, 1990; 1992b; in press; Saariluoma & Hohlfeld, 1994).

Apperceptive errors are particularly clearly demonstrated in experiments in which chess players cannot solve a problem simply because the position entails familiar but incorrect continuation. The familiar line attracts the attention of the subjects so that only the elimination of the decoy possibility makes the correct solution apparent to many of them (Saariluoma, 1990; 1992b; Saariluoma & Hohlfeld, 1994). As the solution in the experimental and control groups was one and the same, and as no secondary tasks were used, memory or subsystem overload can not be a plausible explanation. Nevertheless, the questions may be asked whether apperceptive errors are totally unrelated to working-memory processes. The answer seems to be negative, because these errors are very probably not fully independent from central-executive operations.

Experimental evidence has been collected, which shows that central-executive secondary tasks systematically impair chess players' performance in memory-recall tasks (Bradley, Hudson, Robbins, & Baddeley, 1987). It has equally well been demonstrated that chess players' calculation of variations, as well as their assessment of chess positions, may be hampered by central-executive secondary tasks (Holding, 1989; Bradley et al., 1987).

As both memory and problem-solving experiments show clear impairment as a consequence of central-executive secondary tasks, it seems logical that such tasks would block normal information transmission between the main memory systems, i.e. working and long-term memory. In the presence of central-executive interference, perceptual information cannot be properly connected with the relevant long-term memory information. The attention of the subjects is turned to the central-executive secondary task, and consequently mental-space formation is damaged.

When an activated mental space blocks subjects from representing other hypotheses, a situation in some degree similar to that of central-executive secondary-task interference emerges. Processing mental spaces, as with generating random numbers, prevents subjects' central executives from allocating resources to processing other mental contents. Like central-executive secondary tasks, the activated mental space blocks the central executive. This kind of speculation, connected with the empirical results referred to, suggests that the central executive is not unrelated to apperception, although it has little to do with the organisation of mental contents.

De Groot (1965; 1966) and Newell and Simon (1972) both observed that chess players normally relate small sequences of moves from the initial position onwards; then they return to the beginning and start with a new episode. The key problem concerns the memory mechanisms required in episodic shifts. As the actual mental transformation required within one episode takes place in visuo-spatial working memory, it is logical to interpret impairment in chess players' thinking as a consequence of central-executive secondary tasks, and activated problem space partly in terms of central-executive resource allocation. When they begin a new episode their memory must reallocate memory resources to that episode, and, because resource allocation is one major task of the central executive, its blocking should specifically affect episodic shifts (Baddeley, 1986). This blocking would thus be one source of memory-originated thought errors.

CO-OPERATION OF WORKING MEMORY AND LONG-TERM MEMORY

The active role of the central executive immediately raises a subsequent question. This concerns the role of co-operation and co-ordination of major memory systems in memory-originated thought errors. Fortunately, at the same time as the functions of working memory in adversary problem-solving have been understood in greater detail, substantial improvement in understanding co-operation among memory systems has been achieved and, as a consequence, a new memory structure, long-term working memory, has emerged.[1]

Originally it was thought that all information relevant to maintain a problem-solving process was stored in working memory. However, Charness (1976) noticed in recall tasks that chess players do not store chess positions in their working memory, but rather in their long-term memory. His findings were confirmed very swiftly by a number of authors with very different experimental evidence (Frey & Adesman, 1976; Goldin, 1978; 1979; Lane & Robertson, 1979).

These anomalies, in a Kuhnian (1962) sense, later came under systematic theoretical consideration, when Ericsson and his colleagues started to develop a new way of thinking about experts' use of memory. This work has very evidently shown that when experts carry out some specific task, they do not store task-relevant information directly in their ordinary long-term memory. Such information is rather stored in a retrieval structure that operates a kind of intermediate "cache" memory called the long-term working memory, which is located somewhere between long-term memory and short-term working memory (Chase & Ericsson, 1981; 1982; Ericsson & Kintsch, 1995; Ericsson & Polson, 1988; Ericsson & Staszewski, 1989).

---

[1] I will not attempt to explain the details of long-term working memory, because Anders Ericsson has written on the topic in this book. I just wish to raise some issues which are very relevant in adversary problem-solving.

Long-term working memory is very important in chess players' information-processing. Experiments with blindfold players in particular have provided us with important information about long-term working memory and its role in chess players' thinking. Blindfold chess players do not see the board or the pieces, and the moves are conveyed to them verbally by giving the names of the pieces and the board co-ordinates of the squares from and to which the pieces move (e.g. queen d7–d5). As players often play 10–30 blindfold games simultaneously, the memory load in these experiments is very high and therefore blindfold chess is a very suitable task in which to study expertise effects on remembering (see Holding, 1985, for records). Indeed, all empirical studies so far have shown that very skilled chess players are superior to novices and medium-level players in this task (Binet, 1896/1966; Cleveland, 1907; Fine, 1965; Saariluoma, 1991b).

Strong players may follow and play 10, or even more, blindfold games without making severe errors. Obviously, a memory load of more than 10,000 piece locations and several hundred moves is far too much to be stored in the working memory. There is empirical evidence to show that the storage of games cannot be interfered with by any short-term working-memory secondary tasks such as the Brown–Peterson paradigm when the immediate elaboration phase is over (Brown, 1958; Peterson & Peterson, 1959; Saariluoma, 1992a). This means that the chess-specific information required in blindfold play is stored in a long-term memory-retrieval structure.

Interestingly, chess players' experience of blindfold chess does not entail all the games at one time but only part of one single game (Fine, 1965). Indeed, they seem to focus on one mental space at the time. This means that their representation of a chess position has a functional figure (Saariluoma, 1991b). This functional figure contains one mental space and the pieces relevant to it on the chessboard. This is important because it shows that the rest of the information relevant in that position, e.g. other parts from the active mental space, is stored in long-term working memory, while the active one is manipulated in working memory.

Consequently, one central function of long-term working memory in chess players' thinking is to store temporarily non-processed but already discovered episodes (cf. Newell & Simon, 1972). When they solve a problem, they normally generate from one to six different episodes (de Groot, 1965). Only one of these is processed at a time, and the rest are kept in long-term memory, which presumably means long-term working memory (Ericsson & Kintsch, 1995).

The "capacity paradox" of chess experts' cognition supports this interpretation (Saariluoma, 1995). Capacity paradox means that strong chess players generate very small episodes—around 5–10 moves or so—but they can follow tens of blindfold games at the same time, which means that they can store databases of more than 10,000 moves. Obviously, storage capacity *per se* is not the bottleneck causing thought errors; this seems to be the ability to manipulate just a few moves at a time.

However, if the other hypotheses are stored in long-term working memory, in some cases information transmission within it and short-term working memory must be considered as a source of memory-originated thought errors. This happens particularly when subjects find the correct mental space, but are not able to refine it properly (see Saariluoma, 1990, for an empirical analysis). In these cases the subspaces are moved into long-term working memory, but labelled as incorrect. Consequently, attention is turned to a really incorrect alternative, which means that time and processing resources are no longer used to refine the mental space with the correct solution alternative. Information-access mechanisms from the retrieval structure are decisive in these errors.

INFORMATION IN RETRIEVAL STRUCTURES

Information in chess players' long-term working memory is stored in retrieval structures. In order to understand fully chess players' representations of chess positions, it has been necessary to investigate the semantics of retrieval structures in current psychology. The basis for this work was laid down by Chase and Simon (1973), and after some controversies the current picture seems to be very logical.

Chase and Simon (1973) observed that pieces in recalled chunks seem to have semantic interpiece relations such as attack (either one of the two successively recalled pieces attacks the other), defence (either of the pieces defends the other), proximity (each piece occupies one of the eight squares adjacent to the others), common colour (both pieces have the same colour); and, finally, kind (both pieces are of the same type, for example, pawns). These chess-specific relations were important because the probability of subsequently recalling a piece correlated with the number of chess-specific relations between the pieces (see also Gold & Opwis, 1992).

The connection between the number of chess-specific relations and recall latencies is only correlational, but in chess it is logical that attack, defence, proximity, colour, and kind are important. Pawn chains, and systems of attack and defence relations, form an essential part of chess knowledge. Therefore, chunks or chess-specific patterns are also functional units, and a natural representational format for chess-specific knowledge in the long-term memory (Simon & Barenfeld, 1969; Simon & Chase, 1973; Simon & Gilmartin, 1973). This is why chess-specific relations make the functional structure and "meaningfulness" of mental spaces conceivable.

While Chase & Simon's (1973) experiments provided solid support for the importance of chess-specific relations in long-term storage, they provide complete information on what is coded about the pieces. In principle, three types of chess-relevant information can be coded about a piece: form, colour, and location. As it is evident that form and colour must be coded to define the piece concerned, the key problem is the status of location coding: Do we represent the locations of the chunked pieces, or do we just represent the forms of the chunks in long-term memory? This question was raised by Holding (1985), when he argued against the importance of chess-specific patterns in explaining chess skill.

Holding (1985) pointed out that Chase and Simon's (1973) estimates of the number of stored chunks in long-term memory were far too large (Simon & Gilmartin, 1973). Simon and Chase (1973) tacitly assumed that chess players stored the absolute locations of the pieces in their long-term memories, and Simon and Gilmartin (1973) posited this explicitly (see also Chase & Simon, 1973). Holding (1985) criticised this by pointing out that chess players can recognise any chess-specific pattern, even though it may be moved one or two squares. Whereas the supporters of absolute location coding assumed that patterns located in two different places on the chessboard are different, even though they have the same form (e.g. white pawns on a2,b2 and on d4,e4), Holding (1985) argued for relative location coding.

Saariluoma (1984; 1994) conducted a series of experiments to find empirical evidence, and showed that the location of a chunk had an effect on its recallability, though its form had not changed. If chunks in a presented position are in their original locations on the board, they are easier to encode and recall than if transposed from their original location. This suggests that spatial location information is an essential part of the knowledge stored in chunks. The importance of chess-specific relations and location information in the recall of chess positions suggests that chunks have a complex structure in which very different types of information are encoded.

This analysis of the contents of retrieval structures has several consequences concerning the role of long-term working memory in problem-solving. The most important piece of knowledge is that of confirming the presence of spatial information in chunks, because it explains the possibility of using memory chunks in constructing mental images. If memory chunks did not entail spatial information and they were merely general schemes, it would be hard to explain how chess players were able to construct active precise mental images and also actively manipulate them while attempting to find solutions to chess problems. The pieces cannot just be on the board, but they must be in some precise locations so that representation can make chess-specific sense. Long-term memory chunks with location information explain how the generation of chess images is possible.

The connection between memory-structure content and thinking can perhaps be seen most concretely in some old results on blindfold chess. In Binet's (1896/1966) study, chess masters were already reporting that they could not remember games unless they understood them, which suggests that the encoding was at a deep semantic level (Craik & Lockhart, 1972; Goldin, 1978). Similar remarks were made by experienced subjects in a study carried out almost a hundred years later (Saariluoma, 1991b). This means simply that chess players build their representations by thinking about what is rational in the games presented. Absolute location coding and chess-specific relations enable skilled players rationally to encode positions.

Experts are better at conceptualising chess-specific problems because they have, over the years, been able to build up for themselves a large store of chess-specific chunks with a chess-specific rational structure. Of course, the contents of chess-specific chunks cannot make any sense in business life. In order to understand managerial thinking one must analyse what is relevant information in that context (Hunt, 1991). Nevertheless, the connection between memory and problem-solving in chess and the general principles need not be absolutely different in business from chess. The experience of business people is also built up around chunks, though their contents are very different from chess. While in chess, space and the locations of the pieces are important, in business life, human relations and organisational issues, for example, may be in the forefront (see Wagner, 1991). The main thing is that, on an abstract level, very similar relational information structures and processing systems are used in both.

THE SPEED OF INFORMATION ACCESS

The final question concerning the co-operation of working memory and long-term memory to be discussed here concerns the speed of information access (Ericsson & Kintsch, 1995). This is a point that is worth raising, because speed is the central factor in many adversary problem-solving situations. The faster a solver is, the better are the chances of beating the opponent.

Research into a perceptual classification of chess players has systematically shown that chess experts are faster than less skilled players in finding task-specific information in chess positions. In classifying positions into those involving check and those that do not, experts easily surpass novices (Saariluoma, 1985). The same is also evident when experts have to search for a one-move checkmate (Saariluoma, 1984). Both of these two pieces of information suggest that expert chess players access memory information more quickly than non-chess players. The explanation naturally lies in the automatisation of information intake (Fisk & Lloyd, 1988).

The same conclusion can be made on the ground of recall experiments. Even novices can learn chess positions, provided that they have sufficient time to encode them (Chase & Simon, 1973). Experts' superiority in recall is thus partly a matter of faster access and the integration of relevant information. Faster access here possibly means larger learned chunks, which enable experts to process a greater number of pieces in parallel than is possible for non-experts. Instead of learning all the pieces one by one, experts learn configurations of several pieces at a time (Chase & Simon, 1973).

Finally, in blindfold chess, experts can encode games provided to them move by move with much greater speed than is possible for medium-level players (Saariluoma, 1992a). This is an interesting analogy to recall, because the stimulus presentation is parallel in recall, i.e. the whole position is provided at the same time, whereas in blindfold chess presentation is serial. (This means that one move is given at a time.) Nevertheless, the learning speed of experts is faster.

These results suggest that the speed of access is one further property of chess expertise that must be taken into account when considering chess players' information intake in adversary problem-solving. Naturally, faster encoding is essential when time limits for thinking are imposed, which is the case in many adversary problem-solving situations. When thinking is time limited, fast information encoding is essential to provide the problem-solver with a sufficiently versatile package of information about the situation. Speed of processing decreases the possibility of errors when little time is available.

IMPROVING THINKING BY IMPROVING MEMORY

Adversary situations are conflict situations. This is why society is not satisfied with psychology unless psychologists are able to improve the general human ability to cope with such situations. In practice, this means that psychologists should be able to decrease thought errors in adversary problem-solving and that a better understanding of the role of working memory in thinking will also provide new means for improving thinking. Unfortunately, the positions of psychologists are not always crystal clear.

It is all too human to believe that brave and good deeds are done by intelligent people, but all misdeeds are caused by adverse circumstances. It is the unpleasant task of psychology to show that adverse circumstances are all too often within and not outside human minds involved. This is unpleasant, firstly, because healthy people do not always like to hear that explanations for errors should be sought within themselves, and secondly, because once intelligent people realise that psychology can demonstrate their involvement in the circumstances, they necessarily begin to think that psychologists should accept responsibility for not being able to make decent people avoid the unhappy circumstances within them.

This somewhat "cynical" perspective on the psychology of errors illustrates the dilemma of a psychologist interested in human errors. It is one thing to show that people make errors in adversary problem-solving, and another to find ways to decrease the probability of their occurring. Fortunately, working-memory research can suggest some ways of improving the use of working memory in adversary problem-solving situations, and the major answer to the social demands is undoubtedly task-specific education.

Literature on adversary problem-solving connects education with chunking, because expert superiority is build up around memory chunks (Chase & Simon, 1973). Hence, improving individual storage of memory chunks by training is a sensible course. The interesting issue is naturally what precisely should be improved in the storage of chunks to obtain the best outcome on a cognitive level. Here, I will suggest that chunks have at least three important dimensions, which should be systematically taken into account in the planning of training for adversary problem-solving situations. These aspects are the number of chunks, their size, and finally the relevance of their contents. If one of these dimensions is neglected, the outcome of the training will be not satisfactory.

Evidence of chunking is very systematic in expertise literature. Chase and Simon (1973) showed that experts use a much larger amount of chess-specific chunks in their attempts to resolve chess problems. They were also able to show that experts' chunks are larger in size than those of novice or medium-level chess players.

The final attribute of chunks, i.e. their relevance, is, on the one hand, rather trivial, but, on the other, very complex. This is why it has not aroused as much interest in the literature as the two earlier perspectives. The trivial aspect is that experts have relevant knowledge, whereas non-experts do not. However, comparisons between chess problemists, i.e. people specialised in solving chess problems, and game chess-playing experts have shown that problemists are better at chess problems, whereas chess players are better at playing chess (Gruber & Strube, 1989). This is a tiny difference with respect to content, but it implies that expertise partly involves knowing the right information elements within the field. This means that some people can practise as much as some others, but concentrate on little, less important, task-specific information contents, and consequently a lower level of expertise is developed in the long run.

Research into working memory seems to offer a number of other perspectives on improving thinking by improving memory. However, methods based on chunking provide the most solid practical perspective. The other perspectives pointed out here, such as information transmission, are research problems rather than practical real solutions. The task of future researchers is to show how, by training human memory, they can teach people to cope better with the complexity of adversary problem-solving situations.

SOME PRACTICAL PERSPECTIVES ON ADVERSARY PROBLEM-SOLVING

Because adversary problem-solving is mostly about human conflict, analysis of working memory could be used to clarify the basis of some well-known characteristics of conflict situations. This presupposes change in the very approach. Instead of searching for direct experimental explanations, one should use interpretation and understanding in discussing the relations between working memory and adversary problem-solving. The reason for this is simple: Practical adversary problem-solving processes are often beyond any rational experimentation. One cannot begin a war to test the principles of how the mind works in adversary problem-solving; one just has to consider what has happened and how that may be related to the known properties of the human mind. A couple of examples may illustrate this change in stance.

Conflict situations may be simple and controllable, but often they are very complex and unpredictable. This is why one should never voluntarily go into severe conflict situations without careful preconsiderations and really good reasons. For example, in Chinese general Sun-Tzu's (1963) famous book, this point was made, over 2000 years ago, by a classic commentator of the period, when he argued that one should not go to war without proper consideration. The limited capacity of the mind makes this simple point understandable.

The complexity of most real-life adversary situations, and the limited capacity of human information-processing systems, easily combine to make severe conflict situations very risky. The complexity of adversary situations combined with the relatively small capacity of human working memory and memory systems in general may easily bring to the fore unforeseen factors, which substantially change the basis of precalculations, and "certain victories" may turn out to be severe errors with fatal consequences. History is full of examples, beginning with the Persian invasion of Greece, in which the apparently invincible side or the foolproof strategy has proved to be a great failure, as a consequence of unforeseeable circumstances.

However, to a psychologist, "unforeseeable" is nothing but the failure to represent a problem situation properly. Political, business, or military leaders, like chess players, may well neglect some essential factors by abstracting the wrong mental space or by going into an overcomplex situation and thus surpassing the limits of working memory. In this kind of situation the unforeseeable is nothing but the inability to represent it on time.

Conflict situations cannot be avoided, because all social competition cannot nor should be eliminated. Companies, for example, cannot but compete, and try to find the means to survive and make profit. When there is an alternative to adversary problem-solving, one must also be alert to the human processing capacity. It is often better to keep situations under certain control than to risk all by making them uncontrollably complex. This was very clearly stated by Bjorn Borg (1984) on tennis, as well as by all-time chess champion Emmanuel Lasker (1947) on chess. Certainly, individuals who can force others to surpass their limits should keep the situation simple and controllable for themselves. By surpassing one's own capacity, one just changes a good situation into a risky one.

In adversary problem-solving, monitoring one's own capacity is thus highly important. Perhaps one famous example could end this discussion. Paradoxical as it is, in adversary problem-solving situations the absolutely best operations are not necessarily the optimal ones. Finding the absolutely best alternative at one stage may be too time-consuming and demanding of effort, thus causing problems in finding best moves at a later stage. This is why the best possible solutions are not necessarily the ideal choices, but optimal solutions may be some reasonably good alternatives that can be found by making a reasonable effort. In adversary problem situations, the principle of bounded rationality is as true as ever (Simon, 1956).

Indeed, optimal behaviour in adversary situations necessarily presupposes acknowledging the limits of human information processing and the complexity of life. The person who is not able to understand these limits cannot hope for success in the long run, because, before long, continuous risk causes failure. Therefore, the person who knows what can be controlled has a better chance of avoiding unnecessary errors.

CONCLUSIONS

Working memory is an essential but so far often unacknowledged factor in adversary problem-solving. The classic names in adversary problem-solving literature such as Sun-Tzu (1963) or Miyamoto Musashi (1983) focus on attentional issues, but have very little to say about difficulties related to working memory. This is understandable, as the notion of working memory was not familiar in their time. Although James (1890), for example, knew the role of working memory, it has been very difficult to establish the connection between memory and problem-solving until recently. Memory used to be about the past, and the present was represented by perception in the ancient tradition.

Attention is easy to experience introspectively. If someone does not notice what an opponent does, the outcome is naturally an error, which looks like a lapse of attention. This is a probable explanation for why ancient thinkers, who relied on introspection, considered attention to be the most vital psychological capability in adversary problem-solving apart from thinking. Working-memory research presupposes objective and often instrumental observations. Working memory is not as conspicuous as attention. Moreover, working-memory errors are easy to classify introspectively as lapses of attention, and this is why the role of working memory in adversary problem-solving was so little acknowledged in classic texts.

Nevertheless, today this role appears to be much clearer, although empirical analysis has still been somewhat dominated by chess players' problem-solving. In adversary situations, problem-solvers generate specific representations, which can be called mental spaces. A mental space is an abstraction, or a subspace, of the total problem space, containing networks of operations by both sides. Mental spaces are logically consistent but relatively small in size, because working-memory capacity essentially restricts the human ability to construct them. The modularity of working memory is also an essential factor as far as problem-solving is concerned. It seems evident that subsystem overload may cause severe errors, though we still know relatively little about the mechanisms behind these problems (see Logie, Baddeley, Mane, Donchin, & Sheptak, 1989).

The small capacity of the working memory can be circumvented by using long-term working memory (Ericsson & Kintsch, 1995). This collaboration of the two main memory systems is undoubtedly a very important mechanism, evolutionarily. If the human mind could use only short-term working memory and not build large long-term working-memory representations, human problem-solving would not be cumulative. The skill of problem-solvers would not increase in the way it does.

Even though mental spaces are very small in size, people can represent and solve complicated problems. They can construct large associative structures in their long-term working memory. The communication between these skill-dependent retrieval structures and mental spaces allows problem-solvers to divide the total representation into relevant subtasks. These subtasks can be represented and manipulated in working memory. Consequently, human beings can resolve one subproblem at a time and nevertheless keep the information required for solving the total problem, outside the interference caused by mental manipulation, in their long-term working memories.

Because the capacity of long-term working-memory representations depends on prelearned task-specific information, the outcome of any adversary problem-solving situation depends on task-specific training. A solver who has learned more task-specific information chunks, whose chunks are larger and thus more detailed, and whose task-specific chunks contain more relevant information, is psychologically in a better position, because the probability of error is smaller.

REFERENCES

Allport, A., Antonis, B., & Reynolds, P. (1972). On the division of attention: A disproof of single channel hypothesis. *Quarterly Journal of Experimental Psychology, 24*, 225–235.

Allport, D.A. (1980). Patterns and actions: Cognitive mechanisms are content specific. In G. Claxton (Ed.), *Cognitive psychology: New directions*. London: Routledge & Kegan Paul.

Amsel, E., Langer, R., & Loutzenhisher, L. (1991). Do lawyers reason differently from psychologists? In R.J. Sternberg & P. French (Eds.), *Complex problem solving*. Hillsdale, NJ: Lawrence Erlbaum Associates Inc.

Anderson, J.R. (1983). *The architecture of cognition*. Cambridge, MA: Harvard University Press.

Anderson, J.R., & Jeffries, R. (1985). Novice lisp errors: Undetected losses of information from working memory. *Human–Computer Interaction, 22*, 403–423.

Baddeley, A.D. (1986). *Working memory*. Cambridge: Cambridge University Press.

Baddeley, A.D. (1992). Is working memory working? The fifteenth Bartlett lecture. *Quarterly Journal of Experimental Psychology, 44A*, 1–33.

Baddeley, A.D., & Hitch, G. (1974). Working memory. In G. Bower (Ed.), *The psychology of learning and motivation* (Vol. 8, pp. 47–89). New York: Academic Press.

Binet, A. (1896/1966). Mnemonic virtuosity: A study of chess players. *Genetic Psychology Monographs, 74*, 127–164.

Borg, B. (1984). *Björn Borgin tenniskoulu* [The tennis school of Björn Borg]. Helsinki: Otava.

Bradley, A., Hudson, S., Robbins, T., & Baddeley, A. (1987). *Working memory and chess*. Unpublished report, Cambridge, May 1987.

Brown, J. (1958). Some tests on decay theory in immediate memory. *Quarterly Journal of Experimental Psychology, 10*, 12–21.

Bundesen, C., & Larsen, A. (1975). Visual transformation of size. *Journal of Experimental Psychology: Human Perception and Performance, 1*, 214–220.

Charness, N. (1976). Memory for chess positions: Resistance to interference. *Journal of Experimental Psychology: Human Learning and Memory, 2*, 641–653.

Charness, N. (1981a). Ageing and skilled problem solving. *Journal of Experimental Psychology: General, 110*, 21–38.

Charness, N. (1981b). Search in chess: Age and skill difference. *Journal of Experimental Psychology: Human Perception and Performance, 7*, 467–476.

Charness, N. (1992). The impact of chess research on cognitive science. *Psychological Research, 54*, 4–9.

Chase, W.G., & Ericsson, K.A. (1981). Skilled memory. In J. Anderson (Ed.), *Cognitive skills and their acquisition* (pp. 141–189). Hillsdale, NJ: Lawrence Erlbaum Associates Inc.

Chase, W.G., & Ericsson, K.A. (1982). Skill and working memory. In G. Bower (Ed.), *The psychology of learning and motivation* (Vol. 16, pp. 1–58). New York: Academic Press.

Chase, W.G., & Simon, H.A. (1973). The mind's eye in chess. In W. Chase (Ed.), *Visual information processing* (pp. 215–281). New York: Academic Press.

Cleveland, A.A. (1907). The psychology of chess. *American Journal of Psychology, 18*, 269–308.

Cooper, L.A., & Shepard, R.N. (1973). Chronometric studies of the rotation of mental images. In R. Shepard & L. Cooper (Eds.), Mental images and their transformations (pp. 72–121). Cambridge, MA: MIT Press.

Craik, F.I.M., & Lockhart, R.S. (1972). The levels of processing: A framework for memory research. Journal of Verbal Learning and Verbal Behavior, 11, 671–684.

de Groot, A.D. (1965). Thought and choice in chess. The Hague: Mouton.

de Groot, A.D. (1966). Perception and memory versus thought: Some old ideas and recent findings. In B. Kleinmuntz (Ed.), Problem solving. New York: Wiley.

Denis, M. (1991). Image and cognition. New York: Harvester.

Dewey, J. (1910). How we think? New York: Macmillan.

Djakov, I.N., Petrovsky, N.B., & Rudik, P.A. (1926). Psihologia Shakhmatnoi Igry [Chess psychology]. Moscow: Avtorov.

Ericsson, K.A., & Kintsch, W. (1995). Long-term working memory. Psychological Review, 102, 211–245.

Ericsson, K.A., & Polson, P. (1988). Experimental analysis of the mechanisms of memory skill. Journal of Experimental Psychology: Learning Memory and Cognition, 14, 305–316.

Ericsson, K.A., & Staszewski, J. (1989). Skilled memory and expertise: Mechanisms of exceptional performance. In D. Klahr & K. Kotovsky (Eds.), Complex information processing: The impact of Herbert A. Simon. Hillsdale, NJ: Lawrence Erlbaum Associates Inc.

Fine, R. (1965). The psychology of blindfold chess: An introspective account. Acta Psychologica, 24, 352–370.

Fisk, A.D., & Lloyd, S.J. (1988). The role of stimulus-to-rule consistency in learning rapid application of spatial rules. Human Factors, 30, 35–49.

Frey, P.W., & Adesman, P. (1976). Recall memory for visually presented chess positions. Memory and Cognition, 4, 541–547.

Gilhooly, K.J. (1989). Human and machine problem solving: A comparative overview. In K.J. Gilhooly (Ed.), Human and machine problem solving. New York: Plenum Press.

Gilhooly, K.J., Logie, R.H., Wetherick, N.E., & Wynn, V. (1993). Working memory and strategies in syllogistic-reasoning tasks. Memory and Cognition, 21, 115–124.

Gold, A., & Opwis, K. (1992). Methoden zur empirischen Analyse von Chunks beim Reproduzieren von Schachstellungen. Sprache & Kognition, 11, 1–13.

Goldin, S.E. (1978). The effects of orienting tasks on recognition of chess positions. American Journal of Psychology, 92, 19–31.

Gruber, H., & Strube, G. (1989). Zweierlei Experten: Problemisten, Parteispieler und Novizen beim Lösen von Schachproblemen. Sprache & Kognition, 8, 72–85.

Hintikka, J., & Kulas, J. (1983). The game of language. Dordrecht: Reidel.

Hitch, G. (1978). The role of short-term working memory in mental arithmetic. Cognitive Psychology, 10, 302–323.

Holding, D.H. (1985). The psychology of chess skill. Hillsdale, NJ: Lawrence Erlbaum Associates Inc.

Holding, D.H. (1989). Counting backwards during chess move choice. Bulletin of the Psychonomic Society, 27, 421–424.

Holding, D.H. (1992). Theories of chess skill. Psychological Research, 54, 10–16.

Hsu, F., Anantharaman, T., Campell, M., & Nowatzyk, A. (1990). A grandmaster chess machine. Scientific American, 263, 44–50.

Hunt, E. (1991). Some comments on the study of complexity. In R.J. Sternberg & P. French (Eds.), Complex problem solving. Hillsdale, NJ: Lawrence Erlbaum Associates Inc.

James, W. (1890). The Principles of Psychology, New York: Dover.

Johnson-Laird, P. (1983). Mental models: Towards a cognitive science of language, inference, and consciousness. Cambridge, MA: Harvard University Press.

Johnson-Laird, P., & Byrne, R. (1991). *Deduction*. Hove: Lawrence Erlbaum Associates Ltd.

Jones, A.J. (1980). *Game theory: Mathematical models of conflict*. Chichester: Ellis Horwood.

Jungermann, H. (1983). Two camps of rationality. In R.W. Scholz (Ed.), *Decision making under uncertainty*. Amsterdam: Elsevier.

Kant, I. (1781). *Kritik der Reinen Vernunft* [The Critique of Pure Reason]. Stuttgart: Philip Reclam.

Kuhn, T. (1962). *The structure of scientific revolutions*. Chicago, IL: University of Chicago Press.

Lane, D.M., & Robertson, L. (1979). The generality of the levels of processing hypothesis: An application to memory for chess positions. *Memory and Cognition, 7,* 253–256.

Lasker, E. (1947). *Lasker's manual of chess*. New York: Dover.

Leibniz, G. (1704/1979). *New essays on human understanding*. Cambridge: Cambridge University Press.

Logie, R., Baddeley, A., Mane, A., Donchin, E., & Sheptak, R. (1989). Working memory and the analysis of complex skill by secondary task methodology. *Acta Psychologica, 71,* 53–88.

Logie, R.H., Gilhooly, K.J., & Wynn, V. (1994). Counting on working memory in arithmetic problem solving. *Memory and Cognition, 22,* 395–410.

Logie, R.H., & Salaway, A. (1990). Working memory and modes of thinking. In K.J. Gilhooly, M.T.G. Keane, R.H. Logie, & G. Erdos (Eds.), *Lines of thought: Reflections on the psychology of thinking*. Wiley: London.

Miller, G.E. (1956). The magical number seven plus or minus two: Some limits on our capacity for processing information. *Psychological Review, 63,* 81–97.

Montgomery, H., & Svensson, O. (1976). On decision rules and information processing strategies for choices among multiattribute alternatives. *Scandinavian Journal of Psychology, 17,* 283–291.

Morris, C. (1938). *Foundations of the theory of signs*. Chicago, IL: University of Chicago Press.

Musashi, M. (1983). *Maa, vesi, tuli, tuuli ja tyhjyys* [The book of five rings]. Helsinki: Otava.

Newell, A., & Simon, H.A. (1972). *Human problem solving*. Englewood Cliffs, NJ: Prentice-Hall.

Nilsson, N.J. (1971). *Problem solving methods in artificial intelligence*. New York: McGraw-Hill.

Peterson, L.R., & Peterson, M.J. (1959). Short term retention of individual items. *Journal of Experimental Psychology, 58,* 193–198.

Reason, J. (1990). *Human error*. Cambridge; Cambridge University Press.

Reti, R. (1933). *The Masters of Chessboard*. London: Bell & Sons.

Saariluoma, P. (1984). Coding problem spaces in chess. In *Commentationes scientiarum socialium* (Vol. 23). Turku: Societas Scientiarum Fennica.

Saariluoma, P. (1985). Chess players' intake of task relevant cues. *Memory and Cognition, 13,* 385–391.

Saariluoma, P. (1990). Apperception and restructuring in chess players' problem solving. In K.J. Gilhooly, M.T.G.Keane, R.H. Logie, & G. Eros (Eds.), *Lines of Thought: Reflections on the Psychology of Thinking*. Wiley: London.

Saariluoma, P. (1991a). Visuo-spatial interference and apperception in chess. In M. Denis & R. Logie (Eds.), *Images in Cognition*. Elsevier: Amsterdam.

Saariluoma, P. (1991b). Aspects of skilled imagery in blindfold chess. *Acta Psychologica, 77,* 65–89.

Saariluoma, P. (1992a). Visuo-spatial and articulatory interference in chess players' information intake. *Applied Cognitive Psychology, 6,* 77–89.

Saariluoma, P. (1992b). Error in chess: Apperception restructuring view. *Psychological Research, 54*, 17–26.

Saariluoma, P. (1994). Location coding in chess. *Quarterly Journal of Experimental Psychology, 47A*, 607–630.

Saariluoma, P. (in press). *Chess players thinking: Cognitive psychological approach.* London: Routledge.

Saariluoma, P., & Hohlfeld, M. (1994). Chess players' long-range planning. *European Journal of Cognitive Psychology, 6*, 1–22.

Saariluoma, P. (1995). *Chess players' thinking.* London: Routledge.

Simon, H.A. (1956). Rational choice and the structure of the environment. *Psychological Review, 63*, 129–138.

Simon, H.A. (1974a). How big is a chunk? *Science, 183*, 482–488.

Simon, H.A. (1974b). The psychology of "losing move" in a game of perfect information. *Proceedings of National Academy of Sciences, USA, 71*, 2276–2279.

Simon, H.A. (1977). *Models of discovery.* Dordrecht: Reidel.

Simon, H.A., & Barenfeld, M. (1969). Information-processing analysis of perceptual processes in problem solving. *Psychological Review, 76*, 473–483.

Simon, H.A., & Chase, W.G. (1973). Skill in chess. *American Scientist, 61*, 394–403.

Simon, H.A., & Gilmartin, K. (1973). A simulation of memory for chess positions. *Cognitive Psychology, 5*, 29–46.

Stout, G.F. (1896). *Analytic Psychology.* Macmillan: New York.

Sun-Tzu (1963). *The art of war.* Oxford: Oxford University Press.

von Neumann, J., & Morgenstern, O. (1944). *A theory of games and economic behaviour.* Princeton, NJ: Princeton University Press.

Voss, J.F., Wolfe, C.R., Lawrence, J.A., & Engle, R. (1991). From representation to decision: An analysis of problem solving. In R. J. Sternberg & P. French (Eds.), *Complex problem solving.* Hillsdale, NJ: Lawrence Erlbaum Associates Inc.

Wagner, R.K. (1991). Managerial problem solving. In R.J. Sternberg & P. French (Eds.), *Complex problem solving.* Hillsdale, NJ: Lawrence Erlbaum Associates Inc.

Watkins, M.J. (1977). The intricacy of memory span. *Memory and Cognition, 5*, 529–534.

Wundt, W. (1880). *Logik, I* [Logic]. Stuttgart: Ferdinand Enke.

CHAPTER EIGHT

Development of Processing Capacity Entails Representing More Complex Relations: Implications for Cognitive Development

Graeme S. Halford
University of Queensland, Australia

Capacity has proved a difficult and controversial topic, in both cognition and cognitive development. The question of whether processing capacity changes with age has been particularly intractable in cognitive development, and for approximately three decades there have been two, apparently irreconcilable, schools of thought. Some theorists have proposed that growth in processing capacity or efficiency is a factor that has a major explanatory role in cognitive development (Case, 1985; Halford, 1993; McLaughlin, 1963; Pascual-Leone, 1970). There is no suggestion that capacity carries the whole explanatory burden, but that it is an enabling factor that interacts with knowledge acquisition through experience. Other theorists have argued that growth in capacity has no role in cognitive development, and place the whole explanatory burden on acquisition and organisation of knowledge (Carey, 1985; Chi & Ceci, 1987).

One reason for the relatively slow progress on this issue is the difficulty of the methodology required, which has been discussed elsewhere (Halford, 1993, Chapter 3). However, another reason is that the nature of processing capacity itself has not been well defined, so it has been difficult to specify precisely what is expected to develop if capacity changes with age. My main purpose in this chapter will be try to shed some light on this question. I will suggest an alternative definition of processing capacity, and then suggest that the issue of whether capacity changes with age can be redefined in a way that clarifies some earlier issues.

I will suggest that conceptual complexity can be defined in terms of the number of independent dimensions that need to be represented in order to process a particular task. This constitutes a departure from previous approaches, which tend to define working-memory capacity in terms of the number of elements that can be stored for later processing. We will then argue that growth in processing capacity entails differentiating representations so more dimensions can be processed. I will also outline Parallel Distributed Processing (PDP) models, which help to explain why the number of dimensions that can be processed in parallel is limited, and then I will consider how processing capacity might increase with age.

CONCEPTUAL COMPLEXITY

It is important to note first of all that complexity is not synonymous with difficulty: Tasks can be difficult for many reasons besides their complexity. For example, someone can fail a task for lack of knowledge or strategies, unavailability of the correct hypothesis, poor motivation, etc. Attempts have been made to quantify the complexity of tasks by using the number of levels of a subroutine or goal hierarchy. That is, more complex tasks are those in which more subgoals have to be satisfied before the top goal can be reached (Case, 1985). The problem, however, is that, as Campbell and Bickhard (1992) have pointed out, subroutine hierarchies are not intrinsically constrained, and the number of levels depends on the way the process is programmed, or modelled. Another problem, as I have pointed out elsewhere (Halford, 1993), is that if a task is broken into smaller steps, this reduces processing load, but according to the levels of embedding metric, it becomes more difficult, because there are more subgoals. There is also doubt as to whether subroutines are a good way to represent human cognitive processes (Rumelhart & McClelland, 1986). Overall, it seems reasonable to say that the number of levels of embedding in a subroutine or goal hierarchy does not provide a satisfactory metric.

According to our alternative approach, the processing load for any step in a task is determined by the number of dimensions that must be represented in order to make the decisions required for that step. The approach is underwritten to some extent by the work of Phillips, Halford, and Wilson (1995) showing that concepts, and symbolic processes generally, can be conceptualised as processing of relations. Data structures, such as propositions, lists, and trees, can be represented as relational systems, so a metric based on complexity of relations has wide application. More complete definitions of each level of relational complexity are given elsewhere (Halford, 1993; Halford, Wilson, & Phillips, in press).

The number of entities related, or the number of arguments of the relation, corresponds to the number of dimensions in the concept. The reason is that each argument of a relation can be instantiated independently of the others, and therefore constitutes a separate source of variation or dimension. For example, the relation LARGER (-,-) has two arguments, which can be instantiated in a variety of ways, such as LARGER (elephant, dog), LARGER (rat, mouse), LARGER (mountain, mole-hill), and so on. Because each argument slot can be instantiated in a number of ways, each argument is a separate source of variation (i.e. a dimension). More generally, a relation is a set of points in n-dimensional space, so a unary relation is a region in one-dimensional space, a binary relation is a region in two-dimensional space, and so on. Dimensionality is similar to the idea of degrees of freedom; that is, the number of independent sources of variation in a particular system.

Processing capacity

Capacity has often been identified with short-term memory span, because of the memory theory of Atkinson and Shiffrin (1968), which implied that short-term memory was the workspace of thinking. However, as Baddeley (1990) has pointed out, there is little evidence to support this proposition, and there is considerable evidence that contradicts it. An extensive literature on working memory shows that there is little interference between various cognitive processes, such as decision-making or reasoning, and a concurrent short-term memory task. See Baddeley (1990) or Halford (1993, Chapter 3) for reviews. If short-term memory were the workspace of thinking, such interference would be expected. It seems more likely, therefore, that short-term memory span depends, at least partly, on a specialised system, which Baddeley (1990) calls the phonological loop, and which is distinct from the central processor.

Case (1985) has argued that working memory comprises a single resource, Total Processing Space (TPS), which can be flexibly allocated to processing or operating space (OS) or to storage (Short Term Storage Space, or STSS). Thus, TPS = OS + STSS in Case's system. TPS is constant over age, and OS decreases as processing becomes more efficient, thus making more of the TPS available for STSS. In this way, Case explains a large variety of phenomena, including the growth of short-term memory span with age. However, this formulation is inconsistent with working-memory research, which shows that it is not a unitary system, but has a number of distinct components. Therefore the trade-off between OS and STSS predicted by Case's model simply does not occur, and the phenomena that Case adduces to support his position can be more parsimoniously explained in other ways (Halford, Maybery, O'Hare, & Grant, 1994).

It is important that processing capacity should be distinguished from storage capacity. Working memory is sometimes used to refer to information stored in short-term memory for use in later problem-solving steps, but not being currently processed. Ability to retain such information depends on storage capacity, but not on processing capacity. However, when we decide that the sum of 38 and 94 is 132, the addends actively constrain the decision, and are not simply stored. The capacity required to enable those constraints to be resolved in one decision is a *processing* capacity. The term "processing capacity" should be used for information that is currently entering into some kind of reasoning, decision-making, or other computational process. The term "storage capacity" should be used for information stored for later processing. Working memory is a generic term that includes both.

Relations and capacity

I propose that the number of dimensions provides a good complexity metric for higher cognitive processes, and that there is a limit on the number of dimensions that can be processed in parallel. This is based on the idea, outlined earlier, that complexity is defined by the number of entities that are related, or number of arguments to a relation. Thus the constraints between addends and sum in the problem 38 + 94 = 132 can be expressed as the ternary relation + (added, addend, sum). Orders of constraint, a measure of complexity, can be represented by the complexity of the corresponding relations, which in turn correspond to dimensionality. First, I will consider relations.

A relation is a binding between a relation symbol or predicate R, and one or more arguments, $a, b, .., n$. An n-ary relation $R^n(a, b, .., n)$ is a subset of the cartesian product $S_a \times S_b \times . S, n$, and is a set of points in n-dimensional space. It is a set of ordered n-tuples $\{ .. (a, b, .. n) .. \}$ such that $R(a, b, . n)$ is true. The number of arguments N, corresponds to the number of dimensions in the space defined by the relation, and provides a measure of relational complexity. I will define four levels of dimensionality as follows:

A unary relation $R^1(a)$ has one argument, and is a set of points in one-dimensional space. It can be interpreted as an attribute-value binding (LARGE(dog) assigns dog to that region of the size dimension that corresponds to large things), as variable-constant bindings (e.g. HEIGHT(3–metres)), actions (e.g. RAN(Tom)), or as class membership (e.g. ANIMAL(horse)).

Binary relations $R^2(a, b)$ have two arguments, each of which can be instantiated in any of a number of ways (e.g. LARGER(a, b) has two arguments which can be instantiated as LARGER(horse, dog),.. LARGER(mountain, mole-hill), etc.) A binary relation is a set of points in two-dimensional space. Univariate functions, and unary operators are special cases of binary relations (Halford & Wilson, 1980). Ternary relations $R^3(a, b, c)$ are three-dimensional. Bivariate functions and binary operations are special cases. Quaternary relations $R^4(a, b, c, d)$, are four-dimensional (e.g. proportion $a/b = c/d$).

The four levels of relation, unary to quaternary, will suffice for present purposes to define variations in conceptual complexity. Our next step is to relate them to what is known about complexity from other sources.

ESTIMATING PROCESSING CAPACITY

Miller (1956) suggested that adult humans process about seven "chunks" of information at one time, where chunks are independent units of information of arbitrary size. Both the letter "C" and the word "CAT" (if the letters are integrated into a single unit) constitute one chunk, although they represent very different amounts of information. The concept of a chunk has continued to be important, but the "magical number 7" has encountered difficulties (Baddeley & Hitch, 1974; Baddeley, Thomson, & Buchanan, 1975; Schweickert & Boruff, 1986).

There is more recent evidence that between three and five items of information are processed concurrently. Broadbent (1975) found that, in recall, items were grouped in sets of approximately three or four, suggesting that they were processed by a system that had a capacity of three to four items. In addition, Fisher (1984) found four items (range three to five) were processed jointly in visual scanning, and Halford, Maybery, and Bain (1988) found that in memory scanning four items were active simultaneously for adults, and three for 8–9-year-olds. These findings are consistent with working-memory research by Baddeley and Hitch (1974). Despite the different methodologies, there is some agreement that three to five items are processed in parallel.

Estimates of the number of chunks may still be of some help in estimating the number of dimensions processed in parallel. There is correspondence between chunks and dimensions because both are independent information units of arbitrary size. Dimensions are independent (an attribute on one dimension is independent of attributes on other dimensions), and attributes convey arbitrary amounts of information (depending on the number of possible attributes). It seems reasonable to expect, therefore, that the limitation in chunks might apply to dimensions, implying that the number of dimensions that can be processed in parallel would be approximately four for adults.

Using capacity efficiently

If humans are limited to processing four dimensions in parallel, how are we able to process concepts more complex than four dimensions?

Conceptual chunking and segmentation are means by which we process concepts that entail more than four dimensions without exceeding processing capacity.

Conceptual chunking is recoding a concept into fewer dimensions. For example, the ternary relation R(a, b, c) can be chunked to a binary relation R(a, b/c) by combining b, c into a single argument. The relation between a and b/c can be computed, but the relation between b and c cannot, because they are processed as a single argument. R(a, b, c) can also be chunked to a unary relation, R($a/b/c$), in which a, b, c constitute a single dimension, and relations between them cannot be computed.

Conceptual chunking can be illustrated with the concept of velocity defined as $v = s/t$ (velocity = distance/time). If a decision requires that all three variables be related simultaneously (e.g. a question may be asked in respect of a suitable three-dimensional graph "Is it true that velocity equals distance/time?"), then that decision involves a relationship in three dimensions and is equivalent in complexity to a binary operation or ternary relation. On the other hand, it is also possible to think of velocity as a single dimension, such as the position of a pointer on a dial. Reading such a dial does not require that three dimensions be related in one decision. Rather, it involves interpretation of just a single dimension and hence the capacity required to effect the reading of the dial is less than that required to confirm that a three-variable function is represented by a three-dimensional graph. Conceptual chunks differ form mnemonic chunks in that the former compress relations as well as items.

One consequence of such chunking is that it permits higher-order relations to be processed. For example, when velocity is chunked as a single dimension, it can be represented by a single vector, and combined with up to three other dimensions (we hypothesise) in a single decision. Thus, velocity can be used to define acceleration, $a = (v_2 - v_1)/t$. Acceleration in turn can be chunked, and combined with up to three other dimensions. Thus, force can be defined as the product of mass and acceleration, $F = ma$. Conceptual chunking enables us to bootstrap our way up to concepts of higher and higher (implicit) dimensionality, without exceeding the number of dimensions that can be processed in parallel.

However, the efficiency of chunked representations is gained at a cost, because when representations are chunked we lose the ability to recognise relations within the representation. When velocity is represented as a single dimension, for example, we can no longer compute the way velocity changes as a function of time or distance, or both. Similarly, we cannot compute what happens to time if distance is held constant, and velocity varies, and so on. Thus, although conceptual chunking allows us to handle higher dimensionality than would otherwise be possible, it does not allow all *constituent* variables to be related simultaneously. On the contrary, it works only by collapsing some variables and relations into simpler dimensionality, thereby making the collapsed variables and relations inaccessible at the time of decision (in much the same way that fine detail is lost from view when the magnification of a microscope is reduced: Viewing the coarse-grain structures precludes simultaneous perception of fine-grain structures and the relations between the different levels of structure because we cannot, at the same time and through the same lens, see at different levels of magnification).

Accordingly, it would be totally misleading to infer from the existence of conceptual chunking that there is no effective upper bound to processing capacity. In fact, just the converse is the case. Apparently high-dimensional tasks such as "Confirm that the graph represents $F = ma$" are really tasks of much lower dimensionality, because they do not require that, at the time of decision, all constituent variables and relations be reconciled against the graph (without chunking, this task would require the reconciliation of $F = m$ $(\{s/t\}_2 - \{s/t\}_1)/t$ against a graph of appropriately higher dimensionality). Conceptual chunking is a limited way of circumventing, not eliminating, processing capacity limitations.

Chunking principles are therefore as follows:

1. A chunk functions as a single entity, predicate, or argument, in a relation.
2. No relations can be accessed between items within a chunk.
3. Relations between the chunk and other items, or other chunks, can be accessed.

Segmentation is the decomposition of tasks into steps small enough not to exceed processing capacity, typically by using serial processing strategies. Only that part of a concept that is the focus of attention is constrained by processing capacity at any one time. We are currently developing a model of segmentation in the context of complex analogical reasoning (Halford, Wilson, Guo, Gayler, Wiles, & Stewart, 1994; Halford, Wilson, & McDonald, 1995). Complex analogies, such as that between heat-flow and water-flow, can be represented by a hierarchical structure, in which an overall concept, such as that temperature difference causes heat-flow, is represented as a binary relation, without constituent detail. At the next level down, the details of temperature difference, and of heat flow, are represented separately. At any one time, attention can be focused on the overall concept (that heat-flow is caused by temperature difference), or on one or other detail (on other temperature difference or on heat-flow). A related scheme for time-sharing in connectionist networks has been discussed by Hinton (1990).

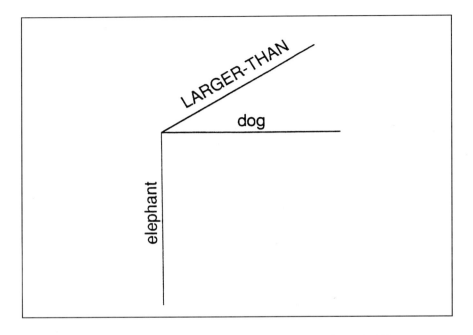

FIG. 8.1.   Tensor-product representation of binary relation LARGER-THAN.

MODELLING THE BASIS OF CAPACITY LIMITATIONS

In this section I will examine how relational concepts can be represented in PDP models. The main point of the section is to show why relational concepts impose high processing loads, and why the load increases with dimensionality of the concept, that is, with the number of arguments, or entities, related. Our work on PDP models of analogies (Halford et al., 1994; 1995) caused us to address the way concepts are represented in PDP architectures, and the approach we adopted led to some natural explanations for the processing loads imposed by relational concepts. I will try to present that explanation here. However, readers who have no interest in PDP (also called neural net or connectionist) models, and who are prepared to take the explanation for the increase in processing load with dimensionality on trust, may wish to skip this section.

The representation of a binary relation, such as LARGER-THAN, is shown in Fig. 8.1.

In order to represent, say, the fact that an elephant is larger than a dog, we need to represent four things. These are:

1. The relation symbol, or predicate, LARGER-THAN.
2. The first argument, elephant.
3. The second argument, dog.
4. The binding of the predicate to the arguments.

In our representation, a vector is used to represent the predicate, LARGER-THAN, and another vector is used to represent each argument. In this example, there are vectors representing the arguments elephant and dog. The predicate-argument binding, that is, the fact that elephant is larger than a dog, is represented by the tensor product of the three vectors, as shown in Fig. 8.1. In fact, each of the units in the vectors representing "larger-than", "elephant", and "dog" is connected to one of the tensor product units in the interior of the figure, but the connections are not shown because they would make the figure too cluttered. The activations on these units effectively code the relation between the vectors.

This representation permits information about the relation to be recovered in a very flexible way. Given the predicate and an argument, we find possible cases of the second argument; e.g. given the predicate "larger-than" and "elephant", the representation permits retrieval of things (such as dogs) that are smaller than elephants. This is equivalent to asking "What is the elephant larger than?", or its complement "What is smaller than an elephant?" The retrieval is achieved by activation spreading from the units representing the predicate (larger-than) and the argument (elephant), though the binding units, to the units representing the second argument (dogs, etc.). The activation is multiplied by the activations in the binding units, which effectively code the relation. Alternatively, given the arguments, the predicate can be found, equivalent to asking what is the relation between elephant and dog. Again, this is achieved by activation spreading from the units representing the arguments, through the binding units, to the units representing the predicate. The representation permits each argument in the relation to be represented as a function of the other(s) and effectively represents the constraints between variables implied by the relation. The tensor-product representation implements a large number of properties basic to relational knowledge (Phillips et al., 1995; Halford et al., in press).

Because LARGER-THAN is a binary relation, with two arguments, it is represented by a rank 3 tensor product, that is, one with three vectors. A unary relation can be represented as a rank 2 tensor product, as shown in Fig. 8.2. To represent category membership (such as that Fido, etc., are dogs), one vector (shown vertically in Fig. 8.2) represents the category label DOG. The other vector would represent the instances (Fido, etc.). Representations of different dogs would be superimposed on to this set of units. Thus, vectors representing each known dog would be superim-

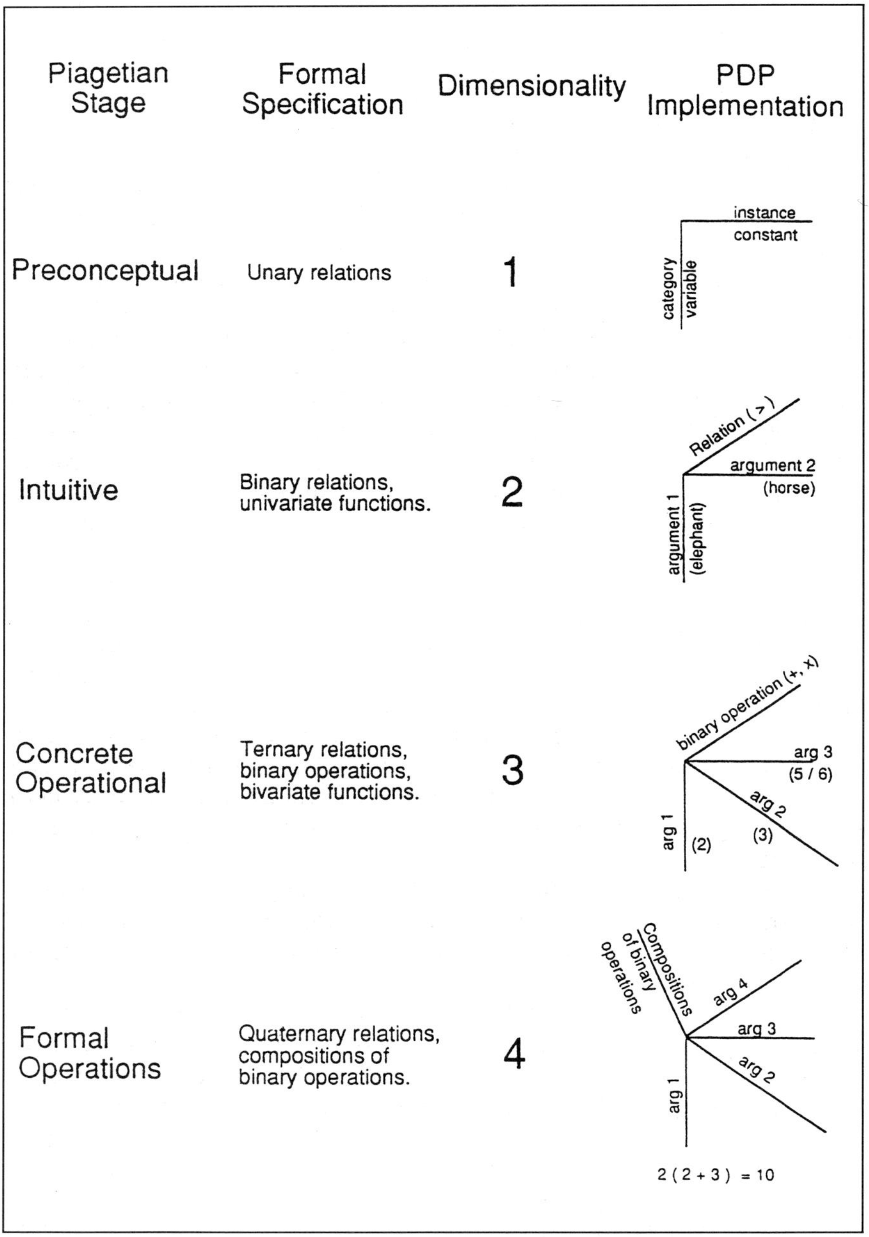

FIG. 8.2.   Tensor-product of unary, binary, ternary, and quaternary relations, together with dimensionality and approximate Piagetian stage.

posed, so the resulting vector would represent the central tendency of the person's experience of dogs: It would represent the person's prototype dog. However, the representations of the individual dogs can still be recovered. Questions such as "are chihuahuas dogs" or "tell me the dogs you know" can be answered by accessing the representation. Note that the representation is one-dimensional because if one component is known, the other is determined. Thus if the argument vector represents a labrador, the other vector must be "dog". Similarly, if the predicate vector represents "dog", the argument vector must represent one or more dogs.

The representation of binary relations entails three vectors, as discussed earlier. It is shown in Fig. 8.1, but is shown again schematically in Fig. 8.2, for comparison with other levels of relational complexity. The representation of tenary relations entails four vectors, one representing the predicate, and three representing arguments. This is also shown schematically in Fig. 8.2. The familiar binary operations of addition and subtraction belong to this level. One vector represents the operation (+ or ×), two others represent the addends (multiplicands), and the fourth vector represents the sum (product). Note that if you know three of these, the fourth is determined; e.g. if you know the numbers are 2, 3, 5 you know the operation is addition; if you know the numbers 2, ?, 5, and the operation is addition, you know the missing number is 3, and so on. (Readers interested in PDP might note that there is no catastrophic forgetting when addition and multiplication are superimposed on a rank 4 tensor product.)

Representation of a quaternary relation requires five vectors, which are also shown in Fig. 8.2. The particular example illustrates the representation of a composition of two binary operations, $2(2 + 3) = 10$. The predicate vector represents the fact that a combination of multiplication and addition is being represented, whereas the other vectors represent the four arguments.

Because a number of tasks that entail ternary relations have been important in cognitive development, I will consider one such concept, transitivity, here. The representation of transitivity requires a rank 4 tensor product, as shown in Fig. 8.3.

There is considerable evidence that transitive inferences are made by integrating premises that represent binary relations into an ordered set of three elements, or ternary relation (Halford, 1993; Sternberg, 1980). That is, premises such as a>b, b>c are integrated into the ternary relation, MONOTONICALLY-LARGER (a, b, c). Consequently, it has to be represented by a tensor product of higher rank than a binary relation, such as LARGER-THAN.

A tensor product of higher rank imposes a higher processing load, because the number of tensor-product units increases exponentially with the number of vectors, and the number of connections increases accord-

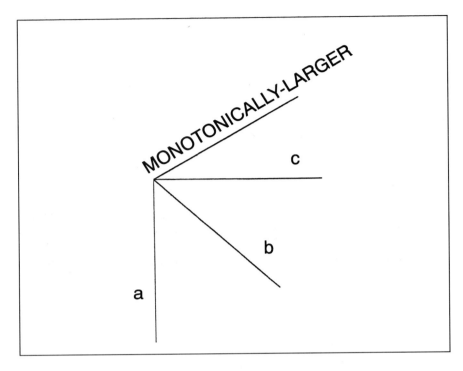

FIG. 8.3. Tensor-product representation of ternary relation, MONOTONICALLY-
LARGER (a, b, c).

ingly. The PDP model therefore provides a natural basis for the increase
in processing load that is observed with more complex concepts such as
transitivity. The representation of unary, binary, ternary, and quaternary
relations is shown schematically in the right column of Fig. 8.2. Unary
relations (one-dimensional) are represented by a tensor product of two
vectors, binary relations (two-dimensional) by a tensor product of three
vectors, and so on. In general, the number of vectors is one more than the
dimensionality. An important effect of this is that the number of units
increases exponentially with the rank of the tensor product. This means
that computational cost (roughly equivalent to the cost of computing the
activations of all the units in the representation) increases with the rank
of the tensor product, and therefore with the dimensionality of the concept.
A more detailed account of this is given elsewhere (Halford, 1993; Halford
et al., 1994).

Computational cost corresponds, in human terms, to processing load.

Thus, the model provides a natural explanation for the observation that processing load increases with dimensionality. This is why those concepts that depend on relating many entities are experienced as more complex than those that relate fewer entities. Thus relational complexity, or dimensionality, provides a good index of processing load. Ability to represent complex relations probably depends, in turn, on the quality of the underlying representation. Furthermore, the quality of representations may be the underlying factor causing variations in processing speed (Halford, 1993, Chapter 3), so the model has the potential to account for age and complexity effects on processing speed.

It appears reasonable to identify chunks, and dimensions, with vectors, because each vector is an independent representational entity that can represent varying amounts of information. Thus, the explanation for the paradox, mentioned earlier, that the limitation in processing is in chunks, that is, in the number of independent units rather than in information, may be that information is represented in vectors, each of which represents one chunk or one dimension. The number of vectors is limited by the computational cost of processing them, and this in turn limits the number of independent items of information that can be processed.

AGE AND DIMENSIONALITY OF REPRESENTATIONS

An extensive assessment of the developmental literature (Halford, 1993) indicates that the complexity of relations that children can process increases with age. Specifically, unary relations are possible at 1 year, binary relations are possible at 2 years, ternary relations at 5 years, and quaternary relations at 11 years. These are median ages, and there is no suggestion that all children simultaneously become capable of processing a given level of relational complexity. Though normative data are as yet very incomplete, it appears that the proportion of children capable of processing a given level of complexity increases with age, according to a biological growth function. For example, the proportion of children who can process ternary relations is probably near zero at age 2, it is 30–40% at age four, 50% at approximately age 5, rising to nearly 100% at about age 10. I will outline those cognitive performances that are characteristic of each level of relational complexity.

Four levels of relational complexity are shown, together with the Piagetian stages to which they approximately correspond, in Fig. 8.2. The rightmost column of the figure indicates the tensor-product representation, to which I will return in a later section, as noted earlier. I will briefly consider the psychological properties of each level of relational complexity. Unary relations include simple categories, defined by one attribute, such as the category of large things, or the category of triangles. They also include categories defined by a collection of attributes that can be represented as a single chunk, such as the category of dogs. Variable–constant binding and object–attribute bindings are also unary relations.

The well-known A not-B error in infant object-constancy research can be thought of as requiring an ability to treat hiding place as a variable. That is, when an infant has repeatedly retrieved an object from hiding place A, then continues to search for it at A, despite having just seen it hidden at B, the infant is treating the hiding place as a constant. However, if hiding place were represented as a variable this perseveration would be overcome. Thus, the fact that the A not-B error disappears after about one year is consistent with the ability to represent rank 2 tensor products developing at that time. This implies that ability to construct representations equivalent to unary relations probably develops at approximately one year of age. We would therefore predict that other performances that require this level of representation should first appear at this time. There should be a general ability to represent variables as distinct from constants. As we have seen, simple categories also occur at approximately this age, and correspond to unary relations. In general, the observations that Piaget attributed to the preconceptual stage appear to require representations equivalent to unary relations.

Binary relations and univariate functions are represented at the next level. These are all two-dimensional concepts (given any two components, the third is determined). Based on an assessment of the cognitive-development literature, Halford (1982; 1993) suggests that they develop at approximately two years of age. They correspond to Piaget's observation that in the intuitive stage children process one (binary) relation at a time.

Ternary relations, binary operations, and bivariate functions are represented at the next level. Well-known examples include transitivity and class inclusion, but there are many other concepts that belong to this level, including conditional discrimination, the transverse-pattern task, the negative-pattern task, dimension-checking in blank-trials tasks, and many more (Halford, 1993).

All these tasks are performed at a median age of about five years of age, but cause considerable difficulty below this age. In a broad sense, this level of processing corresponds to Piaget's concrete operational stage, which can be conceptualised as the ability to process ternary operations or compositions of binary relations (Halford, 1982; 1993; Sheppard, 1978).

Quaternary relations, and compositions of binary operations, can be represented at the fourth level. These include understanding proportion and the ability to reason about relations between fractions, as well as understanding concepts, such as distributivity, that are based on compositions of binary operations In a broad sense, this level of processing corresponds to Piaget's formal operations stage, which entails relations between binary operations (Halford, 1993).

CAPACITY DEVELOPMENT

This argument enables us to reformulate the longstanding question of whether processing capacity changes with age. The question becomes, not whether overall capacity changes with age, but whether representations become more differentiated so that concepts of higher dimensionality can be understood.

Cognitive development cannot be attributed solely to growth of capacity: There is too much evidence that many aspects of performance are attributable, at least in part, to accumulation or restructuring of knowledge (Carey, 185; Chi & Ceci, 1987). However, evidence of the importance of knowledge, skills, or strategies in no way denies that capacity may also play a role. Methodological difficulties in the past have tended to prevent evidence being obtained either for or against the proposition that capacity increases with age. However, there is now a small but growing body of evidence that capacity does change with age. There is physiological evidence of capacity change (Diamond, 1989; Goldman-Rakic, 1987; Rudy, 1991; Thatcher, Walker, & Giudice, 1987). There is also evidence of a general processing speed factor that changes with age (Kail, 1991), and that primary memory capacity changes with age (Halford et al., 1988).

The performance of a child who cannot construct representations of adequate dimensionality is analogous to analysing, say, a three-factor experiment as a series of two-way ANOVAS. Most findings will be a correct account of the data, just as the hypothetical child's performance will be mostly correct. There will be, however, at least in certain telltale cases, higher-order interactions that will be missed. Similarly, the child who deals with an N-dimensional concept using representations of dimensionality fewer than N is really looking at the task through restricted windows. Sooner or later telltale performances will occur that show that the representation was not really adequate. I suggest that this is a good analogue of the role of processing capacity in cognitive development.

ASSESSING PROCESSING CAPACITY

Because conceptual chunking and segmentation enable participants to avoid relating dimensions of information in parallel that would exceed capacity, the key to successful investigation of processing capacity is to devise tasks that require that dimensions be related jointly and inhibit conceptual chunking and segmentation. Interpretation of statistical interactions is a promising task domain because full understanding of an interaction requires that the effects of independent variables be considered jointly (the influence of one variable cannot be determined independently of the others). On the other hand, some forms of interpretation of interactions can be undertaken serially (indeed, no task is incapable in principle of being processed serially), so it is essential that the task procedures inhibit the successful application of serial processing. To the extent that we fail to suppress serial processing, we might overestimate, but cannot underestimate, parallel-processing capacity. With these provisos, the parallel-processing constraint that is inherent in the task means that we can at least determine an upper limit to the complexity of interactions that can be processed in parallel.

Several experiments were conducted to explore the implications of statistical interactions for processing capacity. The only experiment to be considered here entailed assessing understanding of interactions by self-report. The basic idea is that an interaction can be seen, *prima facie*, as a relation. Thus, a two-way interaction can be seen as a relation between two independent variables and a dependent variable, and is therefore a ternary relation. A three-way interaction is a relation between three independent variables and a dependent variable, and so on.

Of 30 participants, 10 answered that they could interpret two-way interactions, 14 three-way interactions, and 6 four-way interactions. The integer central tendency is three-way. This implies that a quaternary relation is processed in parallel. At present, however, we only interpret this datum as suggesting a plausible upper bound on the complexity of interactions that can be processed in parallel.

CONCLUSION

It has been argued that processing capacity should be defined not in terms of the number of items that can be stored for later processing, but in terms of the complexity of relations that can be processed in parallel. I have briefly reviewed evidence that unary relations can be processed at 1 year, binary relations at 2 years, ternary relations at 5 years, and quaternary relations at 11 years (median ages). Quaternary relations also seem to be the most complex that adults can process in parallel, though investigation of this has really only just begun.

Much of the power of cognitive processes lies in processes that overcome these limitations, and these processes depend on expertise. I define these processes as conceptual chunking, which entails "collapsing" a representation into one with fewer dimensions, and segmentation, which entails using serial processing to handle complex tasks in steps that do not exceed capacity limitations. One of the main functions of expertise is to permit conceptual chunking and segmentation to be performed. Thus, capacity development interacts with acquisition and organisation of knowledge. Therefore it is not a question of adopting a capacity-based or knowledge-based explanation of cognitive development, but of working out how the two factors interact. A simplistic dichotomy only clouds the issue.

I have outlined work from our PDP models, which offer a natural explanation for the increase in processing load with increasing dimensionality of concepts. At first it seems counter-intuitive that seemingly simple concepts, based on ternary or quaternary relations, may be a source of difficulty, but this becomes more understandable the more we achieve some insights into the way these concepts are likely to be processed in the brain. Our models are still approximate, of course, but the link between dimensionality and computational cost, equivalent to processing load, seems solid.

The main implication for cognitive development is that some old issues should be reformulated. The issue of capacity versus knowledge-based explanations should be pushed aside: Instead, research could be directed to the nature of changes in processing with age. The hypothesis that follows from the approach to working memory that has been outlined in this chapter is as follows: Capacity development with age entails increasing differentiation of representations so more entities, which correspond to vectors, can be bound together, thereby enabling higher-dimensionality concepts to be represented. With increasing age, representations equivalent to higher-rank tensor products should become possible. The effect of this will enable relations between entities to be considered in parallel. There would not necessarily be an increase in overall capacity, because the total number of representing units need not change. The change would be in the way units are interconnected, which would permit more complex relations to be processed in parallel.

ACKNOWLEDGEMENT

This work was supported by a grant from the Australian Research Council.

REFERENCES

Atkinson, R.C., & Shiffrin, R.M. (1968). *Human memory: A proposed system and its control processes.* New York: Academic Press.

Baddeley, A. D. (1990). *Human memory: Theory and practice.* Needham Heights, MA: Allyn & Bacon.

Baddeley, A.D., & Hitch, G. (1974). Working memory. In G.H. Bower (Ed.), *The psychology of learning and motivation: Advances in research and theory* (pp. 47–89). New York: Academic Press.

Baddeley, A.D., Thomson, N., & Buchanan, M. (1975). Word length and the structure of short-term memory. *Journal of Verbal Learning and Verbal Behavior, 14,* 575–589.

Broadbent, D.E. (1975). *The magic number seven after fifteen years.* London: Wiley.

Campbell, R.L., & Bickhard, M.H. (1992). Types of constraints on development: An interactivist approach. *Developmental Review, 12,* 311–338.

Carey, S. (1985). *Conceptual change in childhood.* Cambridge, MA: MIT Press.

Case, R. (1985). *Intellectual development: Birth to adulthood.* New York: Academic Press.

Chi, M.T.H., & Ceci, S.J. (1987). Content knowledge: Its role, representation and restructuring in memory development. *Advances in Child Development and Behavior, 20,* 91–142.

Diamond, A. (1989). Development as progressive inhibitory control of action: Retrieval of a contiguous object. *Cognitive Development, 4,* 223–249.

Fisher, D.L. (1984). Central capacity limits in consistent mapping, visual search tasks: Four channels or more? *Cognitive Psychology, 16(4),* 449–484.

Goldman-Rakic, P.S. (1987). Development of cortical circuitry and cognitive function. *Child Development, 58,* 601–622.

Halford, G.S. (1982). *The development of thought.* Hillsdale, NJ: Lawrence Erlbaum Associates Inc.

Halford, G.S. (1993). *Children's understanding: the development of mental models.* Hillsdale, NJ: Lawrence Erlbaum Associates Inc.

Halford, G.S., Maybery, M.T., & Bain, J.D. (1988). Set-size effects in primary memory: An age-related capacity limitation? *Memory and Cognition, 16(5),* 489–487.

Halford, G.S., Maybery, M.T., O'Hare, A.W., & Grant, P. (1994). The development of memory and processing capacity. *Child Development, 65,* 1338–1356.

Halford, G.S., & Wilson, W.H. (1980). A category theory approach to cognitive development. *Cognitive Psychology, 12,* 356–411.

Halford, G.S., Wilson, W.H., Guo, J., Gayler, R.W., Wiles, J., & Stewart, J.E.M. (1994). Connectionist implications for processing capacity limitations in analogies. In K.J. Holyoak & J Barnden (Eds.), *Advances in connectionist and neural computation theory, Vol. 2: Analogical connections* (pp. 363–415). Norwood, NJ: Ablex.

Halford, G.S., Wilson, W.H., & McDonald, M. (1995). Complexity of structure mapping in human analogical reasoning: A PDP model. In J.D. Moore & J.F. Lehman (Eds.), *Proceedings of the Annual Conference of the Cognitive Science Society.* Pittsburgh, Pennsylvania (pp. 688–691). Mahwah, NJ: Lawrence Erlbaum Associate Inc.

Halford, G.S., & Wilson, W.H., & Phillips, S. (in press). Processing capacity defined by relational complexity: Implications for comparative, developmental, and cognitive psychology. *Behavioral and Brain Sciences.*

Hinton, G.E. (1990). Mapping part–whole hierarchies into connectionist networks. *Artificial Intelligence, 46,* 47–75.

Kail, R. (1991). Processing time declines exponentially during childhood and adolescence. *Development Psychology, 27(2),* 259–266.

McLaughlin, G.H. (1963). Psycho-logic: A possible alternative to Piaget's formulation. *British Journal of Educational Psychology, 33,* 61–67.

Miller, G.A. (1956). The magical number seven, plus or minus two: Some limits on our capacity for processing information. *Psychological Review, 63,* 81–97.

Pascual-Leone, J.A. (1970). A mathematical model for the transition rule in Piaget's developmental stages. *Acta Psychologica, 32,* 301–345.

Phillips, S., Halford, G.S., & Wilson, W.H. (1995). The processing of associations versus the processing of relations and symbols: A systematic comparison. In J.D. Moore & J.F. Lehman (Eds.), *Proceedings of the Annual Conference of the Cognitive Science Society.* Pittsburgh, Pennsylvania: (pp. 688–691). Mahwah, NJ: Lawrence Erlbaum Associate Inc.

Rudy, J.W. (1991). Elemental and configural associations, the hippocampus and development. *Development Psychobiology, 24(4),* 221–236.

Rumelhart, D.E., & McClelland, J.L. (1986). *Parallel distributed processing: Explorations in the microstructure of cognition: Vol. 1. Foundations.* Boston, MA: MIT Press.

Schweickert, R., & Boruff, B. (1986). Short-term memory capacity: Magic number or magic spell? *Journal of Experimental Psychology: Learning, Memory and Cognition, 12*, 419–425.

Sheppard, J.L. (1978). *A structural analysis of concrete operations.* London: Wiley.

Sternberg, R.J. (1980). Representation and process in linear syllogistic reasoning. *Journal of Experimental Psychology: General, 109*, 119–159.

Thatcher, R.W., Walker, R.A,, & Giudice, S. (1987). Human cerebral hemispheres develop at different rates and ages. *Science, 236*, 1110–1113.

Author Index

Subject Index